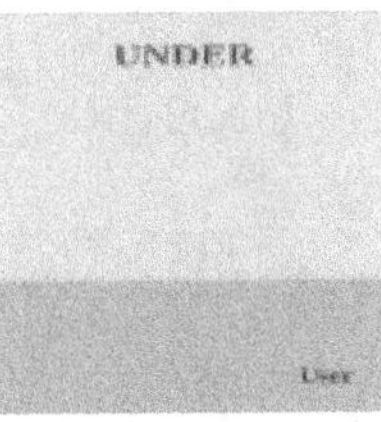

UNDER
User

AF435624

UNDER

THE

SPELL

OF POETRY

SAFFIATOU JOOF

CONTENTS

Dedication

X

Foreword

Xi

iii

UNDER THE SPELL OF POETRY

4

iv

SAFFIATOU JOOF

6

UNDER THE SPELL OF POETRY

13

INCLUDING

INAUGURAL POEM

FOR THE COUNTRY

DEDICATION

I dedicate this book to my mother and late father for their untiring efforts to shape my life.

They did everything possible to make sure that I was educated despite all the hardship in their lives.

I also thank the people that have been so much supportive in terms of my education career; They help me to nurture my talent into a full grown flower that today bears fruits but I would have being happier to give a copy of the book to my father. I pray that Allah grants him "Jannah". I wrote these poems with the intention that many would learn from it and cherish their country men and women and work as team to build a better society.

x

FOREWORD

by Momodou Sabally

"Poetry makes us human. Without poetry and other art forms, the survival of global, planetary consciousness and, indeed, our very existence as a species is called into question." Says author Mary Lee Morrison.

In this anthology, Saffiatou Joof makes a brave attempt to live this ethos; and the work is truly commendable.

It is said in the Islamic tradition that "Surely, there is wisdom in poetry". In this book, Saffiatou gives us a fountain to drink from.

"Under the Spell of Poetry" depicts a real picture of Gambian society in all its glory and contradictions.

The celebration of public figures like the renowned sociologist, Honourable Halifa Sallah and former Vice President ANM Ousainu Darboe among other inspiring public figures in this work has the potential to inspire the young and hopeful generation.

The author already has a voice on Gambian social media as she participates in debates about social and cultural issues. Her poetry will further amplify her thoughts and the voices of thousands that share her views.

xi

UNDER THE SPELL OF POETRY

Looking back on her journey in poetry, I was pleased to note that some of Saffiatou's poems were published by the then budding entertainment magazine "Observer Light", an offshoot of erstwhile leading national newspaper, *Daily Observer*.

It was my fortune to have led that company as CEO and editor in Chief. During this period, we had a passion to provide platforms for creative minds. Saffiatou was one of those young brains to have taken that opportunity to exercise their talents and brighten our world.

Six years later, here we are with the product of a young talented Gambian blessed with the golden gift of consistency and persistence, leading to this gem entitled *"Under the Spell of Poetry"* .

This anthology will be a priceless addition to our libraries and a bright star in the galaxy of Gambian poetry.

xii

UNDER THE SPELL OF POETRY

xii

i

UNDER THE SPELL OF POETRY

PRESIDENT ADAMA BARROW

INAUGURAL POEM:

THE RIVER WE DRINK AS IT GLEAMS

JANUARY 19, 2022

xiv

01. THE RIVER WE DRINK AS IT GLEAMS

As it flows from the Futa Jal on Highland It's The rivers
peace that wil redeem It's the love that disperses to our

streets As the breeze touches the different parts of our
country

To see the little girls smile, As they fold their hands of
dreaming and growing in the lucky land

The old people dance with their beautiful African stories

Remembering the thoughtful tunnels The green vegetables
as we wail for the future with grains

Singing with you our story of our blessed motherland

The deaf and the blind behold, for their chance would arise

The hailing of one voice, a fresh breath to our democracy

When The river flows into our doorsteps, We are hook to
the promise of our President Together we wash our hands
in the river x

v

UNDER THE SPELL OF POETRY

To amend the security forces

Together we monitor the button of our criminals as we
march with various troops

Together we enforce the control of our traffic drivers For
our safety should be of significance The new Gambia, for
our Gambia The youths are the future olives, In whose
creams we should apply.

Futuristic moments of truth, For in your government we
trust.

To ripe us with opportunities for quality jobs, Together we battle against tribalism.

Strengthening the peaceful co-existence of living, For our votes were on purpose.

We pray that thou shal act, to refresh our land into a greater good.

Thus make the hopes of our case fruitful, To reconcile, heal our wounds, Give justice to whom it's due, The fight for corruption in our breeds, To help the underprivileged in our means, When the day begins to decline, 2

SAFFIATOU JOOF

We pray for our feathers never die, Embracing the beautiful cultural norms, Our ancestors have laid the foundation, When we give our economy a taste of freedom, It would enlarge the provisions visions, So give what is due to the Needy, That He may reward those who believe, Out of His bounty, for He loves not those who reject faith,

Giving you a taste of His grace, And we hope the Gambia ship may sail, Thou see raindrops issue from the midst, The river is a stream with strength, Evergreen boundaries as it bangs, For our country The Gambia wil swim with firmness.

3

02. THE BOSS IS CHASING

The voice echoes through the window Imagine a married man doing the hunting.

He's handsome, not financial y broke In his sugar daddy
mood, the voice pulses

"I can protect you with your needs".

Too kind, he smiles from a distance.

On behalf of his feelings

"I was lost, when I heard you"

I withstood, couldn't believe my eyes

"Your body is glowing, mesmerizing.

Your lips are sticky with an endowment Rocket scientists
can't detect the space To shoot out the stars that seem
gluten Your body shape, I couldn't skip.

It's mind-blowing to describe the gifts.

To tel the world about your hips You are classic, he makes
a wish His dream to hit, but couldn't take heed".

The clock is throbbing as he breaks

"May I have your number?

4

SAFFIATOU JOOF

May I know your family member?

May I know if you're single, I'm ready to mingle?

Breath taken to expect the list Overflows of his exaggerated words He smiles to give an aroma of being nice He takes more steps close to my nerves

"I am the director of company X

I can bring you over to work with Y

If my demands are met"

It's a mindset women have to reset.

It's a game; don't al ow to be played The downfal of being weak

Hopeless housewife with many needs Couldn't resist but take a seat The audios are out making headlines, But have the people checked the touch screen The main problem in the streams The position makes her strip

She is lost in the wind.

Before any regrettable stuff

Sugar daddies must learn to retire.

Say No to being a side chick.

5

03. REFLECTION

He gave us knowledge, embodied.

The power to capture each scenario He gave us brain covered membranes He blesses us with nature, not death pages.

The evergreen earth with resources He created a woman from the ribs of a man He gave us the power to love and be loved.

One of the most beautiful things on earth To breath freely, dancing to the tune of culture Colourful we are crafty and not walk barefoot.

The mind to construct a shelter Knowing al the sweet names of our fruits At times he makes life bitter sweet Yet we praise Him, we believe in His prophets.

Remembering the stories of the prophet Muhammad was chosen as His last prophet He brought a religion as a guide to humankind The Quran is a pil ar that serves as a reminder To be spiritual y connected to Him.

He makes man reproductive of himself 6

SAFFIATOU JOOF

Our children as a gift to our souls, He enables us to create a happy environment To accommodate, to train, and change a life He promised us a good garden cal ed paradise Where rivers flow beneath the houses Where man's good deeds get him there But he made death a ticket of access.

Time for the soul to reflect

To understand that we don't own anything We are merely humans with a short lifespan.

Amazing, we look at how the birds fly Hope to live a basic path of life Touching our creatures sharing earth But our hearts are so tight

Full of hatred, the kil ing spirit of humankind Destroying
each other and expecting to live another day.

The prayer that man should make for good He makes for
evil instead of peace.

The love for a brother is fading away.

But forget not the blessings around you.

7

04. A RARE ORNAMENT

It's not a meeting in the classroom Neither a meeting in the
club's house Nor a meeting on the streets, It's a meeting
with striking colours While the pil ows exhibit some signs.

With new bed sheets, they sprinkle.

As the darkness twilights

For the first time, she bleeds Not with fake added resources
On her first night, she pleads.

Afraid of his touch around her His eyes flooded with love

For her dignity, she preserved it.

Like the sunrise, he pumps on her chest Happiness beyond
bound

She is a woman with an origin.

He throws up some flowers

A hug worthy of gold

With a twist on his voice

That whispers, my garden of heaven.

8

SAFFIATOU JOOF

With freshly grown vegetables No more stolen kisses

A virgin girl he has found.

Be prepared to pay for her price Because she is a sacred
element Very rare to be found in the stock of jewel ry
Don't afford to cheaply sacrifice it.

9

05. MOMODOU SABALLY, FORMER SECRETARY GENERAL AND MINISTRY OF PRESIDENTIAL AFFAIRS

There, the Gambian pen

There, he springs knowledge

There, he speaks truth without ill.

There, he has been my role model There, whatever the bridge may be Even so tight to the lion's den There, he would jump and comment 10

SAFFIATOU JOOF

He would serve without fierce to the core He motivates the youths to drink from his straw There, he is like a springtime, making headlines.

There, of wind, in the atmosphere Mrs. Sabal y blinks.

But no amount of spinning can make him shrink.

He believes that greatness comes with patient.

If you want block him in bridge or dam But he would continue to ring like a star.

11

06. TREASURE WOMEN WARRIORS

Lend me your ears, I sent you the message of the century,

Stories of the general scoring found to be them Changing life of women from vil age level A standard for them to access and harness their talent

Women and girls fully enforce from grass roots Nurturing what real hard work means to be told.

Giving you what their women's guitar would rhyme.

In The Gambia won the best national award Heroes.

Can I tel you the phenomenon that they manage to build

Connecting the women of The Gambia under one umbrel a

12

SAFFIATOU JOOF

Impacting and saving the life of young mothers Who once
in their dreams became hopeless Cheer up, revitalizing,
growth seen al over their yard.

Truth beats my heart, they need more support To
encourage that sweat of good skil s, Bring in more women
to realize their potential.

They build more interest to invest in agriculture An
opportunity to have young future farmers That would give
them confidence to face the scale of the market.

Treasure women warriors have been breaking barriers.

Get to check them and give them some treasures.

13

07. LEFT ALONE IN THE DARK

Left alone in the dark

Let's meet at the park.

You mean the most beautiful part of life.

Where adults meet and chat.

Got to see a new face, yet stick to our faith.

Or where children play,

And sing the song of the birds.

No! Places that rock with humorous stories, We close a chapter to laugh, oh! My bad Where adults sit, and "Taal Ataaya".

Tel ing our history of our dear motherland

"Leboon lu pain" , Amon nafie danna am"

Place next to my friends,

Currently in the hood and zipping our cup of juice A country where nurses are not wel paid A country whose soldiers are almost caged.

Glue to my phone, search a channel to choose Watching the news, everything seems not cool.

A country, whose factory is not being praised A country whose resources are hearsays 14

SAFFIATOU JOOF

Lost in the shuffle, people look shocked and baffle.

Where Gunjur cried for recovery Because the fish factory is creating destruction Hazardous to our environment

With overprice of our goods

Our fish have been mortgaged

The Smiling Coast needs to be saved.

Our roads are poor, leading to adverse erosion.

Youth unemployment, growth into a commotion No rapid development up to date

"Leboon lu pain " , Aamon nafie danna am"

Politicians surf on the poor masses' brains Looking for choices, some amending their promises Too many voices for our people to chase Vote for a candidate

Whose future projects come with gains Remember, a bag of rice and oil only last for few days.

Speaking on the policy trails I am hopeful for the new game.

Vote only for that spear of new ideas Whose love for the country surpasses his own gain 15

UNDER THE SPELL OF POETRY

Remember we can't fail to repeat the same mistakes

"Dama jeli doollé, Ndah Muna kas".

To light the candle of our country Some species are stil left in the dark.

16

08. THE ALKAMBA TIMES

The Alkamba Times has arrived, Unraveled the truth
without personal affiliates A young Gambian Time under
rising Ready not to discriminate

But determined to disseminate accurate information.

This is not about defamation

Others say character assassination But a quest for the
people to know their respective country information,

This is our own line, the news time 17

UNDER THE SPELL OF POETRY

Read; watch our unique way of formulating And promoting our population rhymes.

This is our country's pride

A platform to access information according to our rights,

Come on, it is something new

Cal the generation production team The new era of development in terms of news Stretch your back, zip your coffee, click your hands online.

The Alkamba Times.

18

09. TAKE IT AS A RULE

Don't take it like I'm rude.

Take everything as a rule

Avoid being loose, it's not good.

Struggling to become your own light That feeds usual y on your sweat.

It's so cheap; my colleagues did, and earn quick But I refused to strip off what is in my chest.

Don't put the dust in my eyes Stop hoping to see others down Yes! On my knees, I kneel

At night, people sleep, I scroll down My books I crown, my spirit, I fight down.

Comfortable for the little responsibility Fighting for survival is relatively vital in every life.

But without respect for individual dignity, creativity and self-discipline

Mark it zeroes, you're not a heroine.

For our life, people see as a light It's not what happens from inside But it's a hat we must wear at al times.

19

UNDER THE SPELL OF POETRY

My fingers are cross upon the freedom of others.

I count, I fal , I even renounce Never would it stop me from smiling.

I feel my heart rolling with compassion.

The biggest touchiness of jealousy The fake people surrounding our universe So raw in our environment, yet we concord them Process the eye contact, the body language Not even being noticed in our speech.

Yet they lead and they're hard to be seen.

I'm historical y not lost.

20

10. THE DARK PART

Bob Marley, "I want to love and treat you right".

We real y have to mean these words Real love for a brother
and sister is fading by the day And when the night enters,
your brother is in the dark.

Hoping that he's safe in this world But your brother's
hands would write your name with tainted words

When he wakes up, you're the first person that he cal s

You shal smile at him as if everything is alright But tel ing
him, "HELLO BROTHER I hope that you're fine"

But your brother would be the first person to give your
name to the Jinns, to run it in the air The opposite world
that keeps me thinking is love for a brother true within our
hearts.

Unfortunately your brother's intention was to desperately
read your name in the newspapers With disheartening
information For true I keep searching, locked up into the
darkest part of life.

Tue love for a brother is hard to find.

21

11. GIVE HIM WHAT HE DESERVES

He worked from sunrise to sunset He didn't take you as an
opponent But a wife, a sister, and a mother to-be He is
worried about your stomach The food to eat and the water
to drink The clothes to make you look beautiful The rings
and the necklaces, naming you his own Give him what he
deserves

Grateful a good woman, you are supposed to be Even a
shelter is his dream to make you smile He chose you out of

many, cal ing you his baby So respect his responsibilities
And speak to him with kindness And treat him with honour

Give him what he deserves

How can there be a dispute?

How can there be a distance?

Folding his feelings

Throwing them into the bin

Remember he's your sacred partner 22

SAFFIATOU JOOF

So know his heartbeats

And know the language that he speaks And only if you
understand what is peace Give him what he deserves

He's a child very submissive and caring For only if you
know how to teach him a life of sharing,

But the covenant has been broken The secrets have been
spoken

And his voice has been taken

Give him, what he deserved

Our brethren in the popular press Don't ever give up, stop
being stressd But our servants (men) turn to be fighters We
are the world tempting them Our binding shal be truthful
Surely peace shal be our glory Men deserve our beautiful
stories.

12. GAMBIA SCORPIONS AFCON 2022

Singing with the voice of legendary The boys celebrating
strength of gal antry That has been too lonely for the
Scorpions.

But the waves make noise with a beautiful thought 56 years
of footbal with a least victory Even to qualify in AFCON
was a hard school of nursery,

But our boys stunt the pitch with no style of mockery.

Bringing back alive the facets lost of footbal in the country.

24

SAFFIATOU JOOF

Leaving everybody with a big smile of the century To the
boys, I hope!

I hope that you wil understand our tasks I hope that you wil
strive to bring us the Cup I hope you won't lead us
breathless Determination, dedication, I mean make us
speechless as we were hopeless I hope that The Gambia
has a prize Because this is our drive

To make sure footbal is being revived How beautiful!

Our flag wil feel

The crafts man shedding tears of joy The little boy playing
with his toys The toothless grandma singing the love of
choice Bringing old memory's of the late "Biri Biri"

Yes!

Yes to our Footbal Federation Yes to our coaches that
nurtured our boy's Yes to The Gambian people

And yes to our generation that came through to write the
History!.

25

13. SOME POLITICIANS

When I look far and away from the mirror I am al ergic to
the speech being arranged A lot I have observed during
their short coverage campaigns

Their achievements, nobody underrated them So sel your
policies rather than your average The oldest culture that
was found on my page Is buying our trust with a bag of
rice and oil Nothing was new to the stories that continue to
rain Politics of big mouth with less valuable efforts,
Remember, you decorated our imams with foul play And
rose to humiliate them with an eminence space But today

seeking our votes with that cool face We cannot forget the
extremist words being claimed We cannot forget you, too
soon of your display Puppets of the west being honoured
on that crusade they claim

How could you stand to defend the criminals in our
neighbourhood,

But choose to rampage with those found guilty in our
rooms.

26

SAFFIATOU JOOF

When humbleness got lost in our cottage, How can I trust
such an orbit on the globe?

To mount our country with those interludes.

27

14. HATE ON CALL

I'm sorry

To some who said it without any rumours?

To some who hate with no reason Even if you don't do the
act

But write what they say, and I say you have set a seal

On their hearts, guilt

On their hearing, shame

So hate is the final penalty game Okay hail!

The last day, they crave

They behave envious but look plain But they only deceive
themselves For they are fake, in one jail Proclaim! "This,
that, must not, is not yours", you hate

So be at the distance, for them to feel good But nay!
blindly surely they are fools That pretends to make peace

To you reading me, shal we believe, as fools believe?

28

SAFFIATOU JOOF

Each, have a goal on Earth

Hate, I'm sorry

Then strive together with me as in a race Towards al that is
good

No gossip, no bad intention

Wheresoever you are

So be not at al in doubt

After the knowledge has reached Please clean that diseased
heart I feel your pain, in the degree Is eating you with
much greed Our lucks have been decreed

In that I have sent you

Similar favour, so take heed

Hate! Renounce vomited in tears.

15. FAKE FRIENDS

In the witty narrow air

Their lips are sharper than the firearm In a closer range of thoughts They fetch some firewood to burn you alive Do you think they are genuine friends?

Their hearts bounce, upon speaking to you The French smile of love gesture, they behave On your back, they scratch, they show you fake hope A poet husband they even can become While boiling the water that wil burn you At a drop of height, they peep into your life Headaches waving to check out your name Your fal s, they rejoice in their bedrooms For they cry the crocodile tears of support As you climb the hil s, in silence The task of test of time you learn to be private They question the mysterious progress Your channels now are being hidden No tune of measures is known

Words of but how? Come out of them 30

SAFFIATOU JOOF

Where? But you didn't tel them the new norms These are the signs of their complaints Was not enough, their happiness is limited In their drama, death feathers can't dream They wish to see you in their shoes But say nothing, smile, and walk in remix joy Come out with images of the face beat Where the relief of society belongs You wil find yourself not alone Press on the strength of shaping yourself And you wil eventual y lodge in your dreams.

31

16. ALAGIE YORRO JALLOW

Viewers of the year

The writer that drums

In every room, he's being reached The truth that appears like a ring His page is enough for us to drink When he writes, he dribbles with the pen Can't work, his page is more like a gum That I'm glued to, he has a clue, whenever he made a rule

He touches every artery when tuning in the veins Not an empty drain, he's a mega gain Soaring my words into his special day Of the Equator, the freezing ice of #Facebook
32

SAFFIATOU JOOF

He wil lend you his wings

But not even a bird song can stop him Dripping through the cloud and into the deep Like a light fishing being

Capturing every soul, he's close Then you realize your mind has a bearing on him His article chanted, chatted, and scattered, cal ing out the towns and vil ages

For he leaves no story untold He controls, floating out of orbit Heaps of shadows he has rebuilt With a protester twilight sea level His waves are not like unwanted grassroots So natural with his gifts

Even on my sickbed, I wil continue to write your name.

33

17. EVEN THE SOURCE OF MY PEN

So, I condemn the trends,

Our footbal team players chanted So, I vent, I document, I write it out While under oath, "There is no god but God; Muhammad is the Prophet of God".

It gives me torment, heart pain; here I cast the spel And what some want to sel , that we Muslims can't buy it

Our secret is Allah, our breath is Allah And here I glorify that He is the only one worthy of worship

And I wil extend to say, to save us Fame without deen, it's a dead brain Walking on the face of the Earth That's why I don't love celebrities with empty faith How can you realize that you're kil ing your progeny?

It is supposed to be a duty upon us to dig and dig into

What you and I belief

In which we share and that is "Islam as a religion"

We can't say that we are Muslims while being 34

empty,

It's more like a farmer without a hoe.

Allah state that we have to know Him first But we don't confess our sins Before submitting our testimony of faith Then how would you even know how to pray?

He is the only one that can and would say "BE" And

"IT IS".

Allah the omnipotent, the overal boss, The only supreme

None of your sheikhs can

Not even our fathers, or our mothers He is our only source of power And He fuels and blesses you with energy cal ed

"Hamham, knowledge"

And He On, and Off, whosoever that He wishes Stop tel ing me that your secret is from someone else

He is Allah (our lord), the most merciful.

35

18. SHE IS NEXT TO YOUR SOUL

You build trust, not commotions You build maturity, not that big body The man is the foundation

And the woman is the pil ar of the house Most of the
marriages fail

Shortage of compatibility

F9 in anger management

Being handsome is not the greater deal The ideal wife is
the woman with religious consciousness

If she has shyness, that's a good soul Beauty does not
matter, but it is good to be told And being neat and healthy

It's her level of maturity that mounts a full compound

If she speaks, you feel the whole world can't exist without
her

When coming home, you feel that heaven is next to your
soul.

36

19. CELEBRATING A LIVING LEGEND HON.

HALIFA SALLAH

Dear, Honourable, Halifa Sal ah You're the legend that I accord Never been recorded frauds in our court You stream the generation palm tree A man full of perception and not deception means You're the leader with a unique voice That during the political impasse You stood up to settle the climate You're The Gambian Palm Tree

With shoots of fruits that I stil question how we afford to miss it

But your chapter in the struggle 37

UNDER THE SPELL OF POETRY

Shal never be closed in our books I thought much of your famous quotes

"That Seeking knowledge is useful It's not just a tool for darkness but a light in our hearts"

When we shouted for Halifa by force He taps to Halifa by choice

The blueprint of his dignity

Is greatly guided by his integrity Therewith, his depths of wisdom Surpass our eardrum to listen Therewith, your leadership style So affordable, yet our people refused to buy it You're more than a page in our democracy A garden for the generation to harvest Your results demonstrate outstanding You're face brethren

Nearer to our jugular veins

Yet my people afford to miss it Your fight for injustices

You and Honourable Sidia Jatta Imprinted that mission on
our two palms 38

SAFFIATOU JOOF

Expired not, you're a spider in our minds More like a stain
on our wal s You prepared the ground for the evolution of
our generation

Part of it which you enforce clarity And a commitment to
your country Should I tel you a little bit of history?

When he went for eye surgery

His doctor advised him to stay But patriotism couldn't let
him be And this is what he has to say

"Finance is the lifeblood of every nation and he can't
afford to miss the session"

On a scroll folded, humble in his work Witness not, even
an atom of corruption in his traits None on earth can cleave
a thunder But Halifa and Sidia are like a rock star in our

"Xalam"

Yet my people afford to miss it When he does, take heed

Halifa is a full university

He sets a seal in our hearts, 39

UNDER THE SPELL OF POETRY

He's a rare special apple,

That even a toddler cannot disapprove, He retired from politics,

But retired not, in our minds, A fearless man with sharp fruits, A legend in our path, that sadly, The Gambia has missed the chance.

40

CELEBRATING OUR LIVING LEGEND: **20. HON.ANM OUSAINOU DARBOE FORMER**

VICE PRESIDENT OF THE RIPUBLIC OF THE

GAMBIA

It was long overdue that a man has placed his life for our freedom

It was overview your name shal never be erased from our history

Politics can kick you out of our circle But your legacy has marked a footprint in our democracy

You are a whole rainbow

41

UNDER THE SPELL OF POETRY

An enormous mirror in the struggle Not only a referee, a key player in the liberation That fought teeth to teeth up to prison This is our revelation, a champion in the proliferation By grace, you are a name

For The Gambia is your place

By grace, you're a tree

Whose trunks cannot be bundled By grace, you're a bird

That would continue to fly in the jungle By grace, you have sweat

This indeed, has touched the land that you redid By grace, you have revived the people from despair A dictator was found overstay Honourable Darboe played to reset the closet Sorry to the lost souls, whose fraction didn't survive it

It was a huge clutch; your tactics prove a facet Verily your kind shouldn't be missed in our breathing Verily your fight was fruitful for our nation to gain sovereignty

Proceed by grace; none can tarnish your image 42

SAFFIATOU JOOF

Because steadily you grew

Swept them al under the bridge Quickly take a heed, he is like bedrock in the political arena

Some tailoring you to be old

But have forgotten experience is gold Let no heart be depressed no more A father figure that Gambians need to give much respect

Fear not, none sorrowful any more Your records for the rule of law Have left thereof evidence

A good sign of your work

Long live, in the increasing length of your age A man of the elite, an honourable notable shadow Diplomatic person, a king in the practice of law A man of goodwil intentions

Together I salute you and the genuine fighters Together I salute you and the pen writer That inks the slogan of sovereignty Honourable Darboe is a star in the struggle And in my country's book a legend.

43

UNDER THE SPELL OF POETRY

21. THE IRON LADY ZAINAB MUSA DARBOE

(JAINABA DARBOE)

Facing each other on a throne of dignity Zainab, you're a
woman of personality That helps the poor and the youths
with humility Facing each other for the generous work of
humanity

Your contribution towards society, changing the lives of so
many youths

Without a second thought or loss of cost, wil be graciously
written in history 44

SAFFIATOU JOOF

Allow me to recite an epic of your quality A rare ornament
of a gem

You adopt, you train, you motivate, you mould, You
cultivate, you nurture

You initiate you coordinate, you establish you ensure And
above al

Investing in community organizations With a special force
of redemption I raise my voice with the truth I raise my
voice not with the motion of condemnation

But to encourage human beings in your similar deeds

Branded with authentic jubilation and chorus it to the birds
as we breathe

Particularly for society to take your heroism As one of the
best nominations of integrity They said, ' Charity begins at
home And you're the queen of that quote And Gambians
can confess to that choice My words are not written in
deception But an act of a complete vision 45

Representing Zainab's patriotism A zealous commitment based on existence The value and honour of your symbol Engulfed in the hearts of Gambians Shal I order the vocalist to the park?

Zainab our heroine, bonus mark Nobody dares to stop your star

"Oh Allah nyaa dua ying Cairo"

"Fo hakilI tenko, Ning haar jeebaa"

If only we should find a leader We wil choose you and forget another Insisting on your type of celibacy Recal ing the history of her legacy Reversing the records of her generosity A woman, whose gal ery can't be dusted Decode the cassette as a rocket, As the galaxies manifested your prosperity, Thanks to al of your abilities, Done In the name of human development, More wins ahead of your deeds.

46

22. SHE IS INTACT

She is glowing, as she steps in her glorious moment She is fresh, untouched with her classic price She maintains her precious spiritual body His trust grows; you become the throne of his household

Because she refused to give out her dignity for a cheap story

Our culture so rich, we are here to embrace it When she is found intact

The man body wouldn't die

His soul would rise above the sky, as he smiles His respect
grows and she becomes honoured He praises you, and
Allah wil reward you She gives you purity, pure love, and
clean honey These are not my words, but the Prophet
advises This is not for us to judge, even our culture
endorses it

If you feel so much lust, wel love is a choice You can spew
out hurtful words But can't stop any man to search for
intact 47

UNDER THE SPELL OF POETRY

A whole package is a blessing If especial y undamaged or
unbroken The amusement found intact

Be prepared to pay the flower of a virgin girl.

48

23. VIRGIN PEARLS

We have to be careful of how we redeem To reaffirm our
faith and lower our Google lenses The earth is wonderful
with its virtuous moments and lessons

But the most beautiful part of it is a virtuous woman Based
on culture and traditions It shal be deemed necessary

But Islam raises the flag of a virgin girl completely sacred

And different from a non-virgin Completely sealed and
sacred

Untouched, wel armed

Drips nothing but a clean flower The beauty is never being found Even being so lust

One cross of mistake, it's gone Let's save the pearls, it is worth it.

49

24. THE DECOMPOSITION OF NATURE

From the beginning to the end The decomposition of Nature

From heaven down to Earth

Humankind was created, as a blessing to nature From the Quran, in Al Baqara, It was found When your Lord said to the angels

"I wil make upon the Earth a successive authority"

They said

"Wil you place upon it, one who causes corruption therein?

And sheds blood, while we exalt you with praise and declare your perfection?"

Then the Lord said

"Indeed, I know that which you do not know"

Shattered hopes beyond bounds Nature's rights were neglected The depletion of humankind

Towards a curse, we have signed It's already celebrated, manifested and elevated The alteration, the division of humankind In which the human rights advocates for 50

And wants it to be implemented I stand for nature, whose
rights were seized and violated

Immediately exploited, and they want it to be decorated
like an Evergreen Baobab Tree To be a normal saturated
situation To switch to any gender

To wear the clothes of any woman To speak in the voice of
a man To walk on the streets in the uniform of a stripped
gay

To dance in the streets as a symbol of a paraded lesbian

Don't forget, the wonderful gift of nature To have children
on the play ground To have someone in the house that we
would cal her Mum

To go for a vacation with people that we wil cal a family

It's hazardous to nature as a bad deterioration on earth

It's dangerous to nature, just like unwanted grass that
grows beneath the beautiful fresh vegetable garden

51

UNDER THE SPELL OF POETRY

It's an uncivilized human act As the lord created you from
one soul And created from its mate

And dispersed from both of them Many men and women

From the beginning, it was never a man to man None, a
woman to woman

Even the animal kingdom chooses to multiply It's a bad
breath that smel s like faeces in the toilet Hidden agendas
in the calendars When some hail for their pride I calmly cal
them down dehumanizing lost souls That we need to
collectively console Not with our hands to beat them Not
with our legs to kick them Not with our abusive words to
hurt them But mental y boost them to regain their senses
It's not in our genes, a condition where desires can't be
defeated

It's not in our culture, where it has to be cultivated But it
was in our history, considered like mental il ness

52

SAFFIATOU JOOF

It's a problem that choked them Waiting for people to poke
them The silent majority during childhood were abused
The depressing condition in society They felt no gain, they
felt so much drain With so much pain

Society shouldn't reject them Instead, we need to engage
them They are lost in the deep sea They need a boat to
shove a rescue Not with the human rights laws Their
feelings wil be gracefully abused Sad! That they have been
given false hopes Deteriorated their growth into addictions
And want Africa, Africa to embrace their man-made
legislation

A word is enough for the wise Strengthen the awareness, to
be warned before being wounded

Hel broke loose, don't let nature freeze over 53

25. TALENT

One of the brightest gifts

That one could ever possess on Earth Talent

That you could use to become a unique individual in
society

Paying your bil s through its income Talent

I refuse to let it die,

I refuse to let it be like dust in the air.

Talent

It's the only tool that would bring that change we al need

Embodied within our soul

That we can seek to inspire

Sensitize and wave into the generation to respite And so we
watch again

Our gazes at the heights of our talent 54

SAFFIATOU JOOF

Nurturing it to remain not only as a history But a life-
changing mirror on the face of the earth In our arena of
talents

We close the gap of hatred

And open the doors of hope to flourish We watere the roses
of our talents That put our future first

Seeking peace for al

And the holding of grudges for none Talent

Let it blow and grow

Offering a huge hold of hope

Fearing not its redemption

So we asked

How would we possibly prevail over our talent?

When our environment is not that friendly Hail to rise above the environment Draw a new chapter of practising what we love doing And what so many people have given up 55

UNDER THE SPELL OF POETRY

Pageant to an inevitable part For that, the future has given Brave but bold

With goals to scour into the fitted future We are hacking and backing our talents With a flute and a guitar

To touch the string of our lives and hearts We wil not murder our talent like a tale in history We are the chosen ones to remain, to rename And be covered in the hottest tickets of history To you that believe not in your talent Our talent is given birth every day Delivering messages each day

For I am not brushing the cats teeth But glistening our eyes, inspiring the minds So shackle off that shyness

That chain that holds you apart Shooting down with words of hope 56

That our talent turns to be a school of thought For I give
you this poem to learn And start embracing your talent 57

26. OUR HOPES ARE HIGH

Our hopes are high

Gambians aren't the fools

But it takes them time to choose You can't predict people
without getting into the hood

And light up the candles

This is a tool that many could lose Divide and rule that
game would be interim Come December the climate would
change Even the burglars shal be correctly tamed Come
closer spice, reason with time This is your right, hope you
hear my mind Vote wisely

There would be no rain but some would pack their
resources

Get back to the heritage

Our only gate of the election, forget Bil Gates Some
political snakes shal be shocked A rock would be hard to
strike But the victory shal fit the spike A struck undermine,
give me the mike 58

SAFFIATOU JOOF

The clock shal tick the documentary That silent majority
would make history From the distance of the mirror Our
hearts beat the game being fiddled With the trees looking
evergreen Even a blind duck could riddle the wriggle That

patience is a virtue, keep on practising Politics goes with
actions

Life on the street, maybe weaking us quick We forget to
skip, that too much greed Leadership isn't about
continuous ice cream Some signs of arrogance aren't
hidden A natural redeem first detected in the bil ing An
opportunity was available; it was thrown in the bin

It's simply kil ing

All manifested within minutes A behaviour perhaps that
establishes a clear trap Looking up the campaign,
comparing the race With limited knowledge, don't blame,
only the insults could rain

Because Gambians aren't puppets that one could 59

UNDER THE SPELL OF POETRY

use,

That pretending kind of being with al phenomena would
not rise

Our pride al lies in our bal ot So vote wisely, coordinate
tightly, and sensitize kindly

The silent majority always decides the bal ot.

60

27. REFUSED

We cannot forget how it was formed An al iance of
agreement turns to be betrayed We run office differently

We know the truth gave a deaf ear We promise people, make fun of them Offering help while spoiling our resources A missing girl case of no conclusion A drug case with no news of prosecution Corrupt people got redeployment Bribery becomes our norm

We have mil ions to offer, none but a political leader While pregnant women are dying at the hospitals Youth unemployment benefits stop in their pockets This is a country of one person's interest No complaint, hence the cake is on your table An affiliated person is cal ed a friend An enemy of the state is the truthful person Politicians have divided us

Brainwashed our intel ectuals Pumped them money to fool us even more 61

UNDER THE SPELL OF POETRY

Instead of holding the state accountable We are enemy to each other

A change of mindset and a check back to the system.

62

28. OPEN YOUR EYES

Whispering my angelic voice

We are not youth with toothless gums We are the youth with no wrinkles Young fresh and flesh in one uniform We are ready to be crucified; Our country must rise and shine I feel my heart tearing down poverty continues to be modernized

The selfish thief dresses up like a respected individual

While leading our country into a financial crisis The prose
of yielding our future, fish cost goes higher

Fuel wil continue to fluctuate, a country that has no control
of prices

I went to the market for a bag of rice But the goods have
been over priced And yet, this is the country we have
decided Let's open our eyes; this is our time to decide
Apply the perfume, get the drums and blow the trumpet of
change

63

UNDER THE SPELL OF POETRY

Remember, these are the days we wil be bribed and
scooted

Our people wil be given attention just for their own gain

These are the days when our voice wil be heard Our tears
wil be wiped for a few months with chicken change

They are driving nice cars, bade us up to the lake Left us in
the stream, we wil end up screaming and floating alone

They build up multiple buildings and leave us in roasted
poor cottages

There wil be no honey, if we are not ready to taste the juice

Wear the national flag of freedom Run down to the houses
to raise awareness in the region

Hearing this voice of freedom Reminding you of the
package of false promises I did not come to you with a
facet of dictatorship I am here to expose the weak vultures

Don't be mere spectators instead You have to believe that
your one vote can create a lots of change

64

SAFFIATOU JOOF

Be cautious of the vulture that smiles at you When only it
needs your applause in order to survive for a while.

65

UNDER THE SPELL OF POETRY

29. MIRACULOUS

There is a deeper life than people thought And one can't
realize that reality until death comes Let's not be among
those that would be registered as forgotten

One good example is the people that never come back

They never come back to explain what death seems to be
like and

They can't tel us anything even when their time is up

He issues rain forth from the sky's midst Mountain masses
from of clouds The flash of its lightning wel blinds sight
The birds with wings that fly in the air So invisible yet we
breathe the atmosphere In a verse of deep ocean

So dark inside when seen from the above surface But have
light when divers swim inside We can't divert its sources

Yet so fresh when filtered to drink and We can use it as
irrigation

SAFFIATOU JOOF

It waters the gardens

producing crops suitable for consumption Our eyes do see
the sea, our shapes and limbs so amazing

When we are hungry

We rush to catch a fish

Let's not be thirsty for too much life And come closer and
find nothing I look around nature's amazing edible plants
that grow beautifully.

The sea inhabitants of different types of species A baby wil
be formed, with the drop of a single sperm cel .

During childhood, can't do anything But would learn from
the parents language How to talk and walk?

A creation of a human being

The heart shal and wil circulate blood and The entire body
can't function in the absence of blood

If we don't believe in Allah what else should we believe?

The month that comes to renew our Faith 67

UNDER THE SPELL OF POETRY

Unless we become lazy

12 months in a year and make one become glorious
Ramadan becomes full of blessings Reminding us to

become merciful to each other Love sharing, charitable
within our hearts At times, He tests us; we feel pain Being
hurt by words, without bleeding blood I look into the sky
and how stars are being arranged I wonder but He clearly
states That's not Him

Great scientists studied different areas of specialization

Neurologists and physicians

Some even fly on an aeroplane Some are into space as
astronauts Some are doctors and yet He states there is
nothing like Him

If we don't believe in Allah, what else should we believe?

"Al ahu nooru alssamawati waalardi"

From the Quran He then states that

"HE (ALLAH) is the Light of the heavens and the earth.

68

SAFFIATOU JOOF

His light is like a niche in which there is a lamp The lamp
is in a crystal, and the crystal is like a shining star,

Lit from ⌐the oil of⌐ a blessed olive tree Located⌐ neither to
the east nor the west Whose oil would almost glow, even
without being touched by fire?

Light upon light! Allah guides whomever He wil s to His
light.

And Allah sets forth parables for humanity For Allah has
⌐perfect⌐ knowledge of al things"

If we don't believe in Allah then what else should we believe?

Allah is the final goal

Everything belongs to Him

Even the pen that I write poetry for you to read He controls the mind and the heart it sources from.

30. THE JOURNEY OF MARRIAGE

There wil be a time that we wil own There wil be a time that we cannot fold There wil be a time that you cannot stop or hold And when that time comes, you wil say YES!

That was decreed by Allah

And there wil be a time that wil be retold Like a vain tale told

I know it wil be hard to explain But it wil be explained

And parents wil come together to listen To listen to their beautiful sons and daughters Singing a song from their hearts that was stolen by poetry

Listen to tales ringing in their ears Like a chiming bel

This is unbelievable, unimaginable That was what we always needed A motivation, a holy nation, not envious friends Parents wil be told, "Behold"

This is the most amazing news that we have ever breathed from the nose

SAFFIATOU JOOF

Then mature imams wil start to play their roles.

Like that of the #Prophet Muhammad (PBUH) That shows
and taught every example that he was told by Allah

The saints and saintly imams wil be gathered in a circle

Honourable Old learned bald heads Wearing beautiful
countless masks Wil then stand up to express their happy
souls Then an imam wil rise up

I'm not a tale tel er

But I'l tel this tale

Who else wil tel this tale?

Old wisdoms inviting new wisdoms to their nation How
they dreamt that they would listen That has an ear alone

Oh words were lightly spoken

They advised, choose your companions wisely Don't be so
free with every sort of company With every Jack and Jil

They learn, but man is a fool and youth is naive Hearing it
now

71

UNDER THE SPELL OF POETRY

I have sighed for those young men They have found the
path their own feet cannot find But seeing them now has
made my grief less bitter As they listen in gentleness

And learn in roughness

O don't miss the happy ending of this story Because this is
the beginning of this holy journey DUET BY NNA'
KALA AND WALAA

72

31. THIS WORLD

Say!

Does man think that his decaying broken bones wil not be
assembled?

Does man think that there is a place to escape the hel fire?

Allah has prepared chains

Shackles and a blaze

Stop expecting that there wil be backbreaking This world is
dazzle

Desires are like lanes

And the moon that darkens

Some faces that day

Wil be like radiant and get contorted To your lord that day
wil be the procession?

Does man think that he wil be left neglected?

68

Had he not been a sperm from semen emitted?

Then he was a clinging clot

And Allah created

Woe to the people

That can't stop swaggering in pride Abusing women and children free of charge 73

UNDER THE SPELL OF POETRY

Smoking marijuana and cocaine Like that was desired for your life Beating and insulting children, like we have nobody to fight for our rights

Sel ing young girls and boys as slaves because of our own interest in this life

Some men think that, they are strong and brave So they can marry many wives

Remember Allah states

You have to give them equal rights Clothing and feeding

To be total y sufficient for al wives We term to take things so slight and Hurt people anyhow

Blood relationships don't exist We cut the chain and resist

Backbiting and gossiping every day Bleaching and pretending, false hair extension You are buying and fixing nails Like you are guarantee of living another life Sister don't take that so slight Because Allah states that

74

He cursed Muslim women

That got their hair extended

Do not be afraid

To accept truth and change

We are al imperfect

The cervical cancer is under rise Women have to be
sensitized

Women, men and children are dying of poverty Because
our leaders are corrupt humans of al types That goes for a
war every time The popularity of poverty

Hunger and drought,

That made us lose our respect and dignity Involving in
kidnapping and rape Oh! The people of this world

Allah swears by the day of resurrection He swears by the
reproaching soul The Day of Judgment is the truth.

75

32. THE REVELATION

I'm sending the revelation

Let's do the dissemination

Because this is the real information Hel broke loose

Death always broke the constitution He never delayed no matter the condition Let's start the communication We al need dedication and determination For no more complications

No time for condemnation

Make more fruitful positive production Oh death, you are one of the sensations That has no limitations

Taking us without any alert of aviation Hel broke loose

Let's cook the goose

This is my agitation

We don't know about our final destination This is hidden like gravitation Be focused like today is the preparation 76

SAFFIATOU JOOF

I'm feeling the situation

The world is screwed into series of reduction Don't we feel the situation?

We are al crying out of affection Without that much connection

But humanity swings

It is rough and tough

But we always have an option

Our service police

Department colleagues

We are al feeling the same situation So to you our
generation

Let's work harder to achieve the dreams To make sure
we're al clean

Seek the Almighty's attention Let's bow down to our knees

He is full of mercy and manifestation This is more than
magnetization Magnificent, an opportunity door is open
For the century of purification Repentance is the only door
for He owns the glorification

77

UNDER THE SPELL OF POETRY

Ya Rahman, Ya Rahim, may you have mercy on our souls

A special tribute to al the departed souls 78

33. ADVICE TO THE YOUNG GENERATION

The heart feels shocked

The mind is heavy like a truck The rocks hold the
mountains

But the body is nothing other than dust I hope you don't
rush

Before crossing to build the trust Dear Women,

You see our exposure

Our body cute in shape

Our lips so leeched like lake That when we talk and walk

Shaitan whispers like dates It is not meant for every folk
But someone that would be your gate Real men not
hypnosis like fake A talkative who would tel you his uncle
is named Jane

Subtitles your mind

Give the heart to a man that would title your life with
Rosemary

He's wasting your Time

79

UNDER THE SPELL OF POETRY

For the naughty conversations No seed deems fruits, grows
none grains For even education he's stick up ideas of no
gain Talking about classic

when his thoughts are al glass sick.

80

34. DEAR YOUNG MEN

I hope that you choose

Don't get it loose, because we aren't the same But true,
some women are being fooled By the looks and the tal
dude We like the fame

We chase the dude when money is seen al around you

Open your eyes, your children deserve a good mother

Not a daughter that would come destroying your hood

Sailor with you when it was nice and cool But leave you
the moment the money is forecast frozen

This is my doze, let material be the least to build your love

Before regretting why you fel in love We rub you during
the course

Some of us don't see your love but How your pocket looks
and run indoors Whenever I write

81

UNDER THE SPELL OF POETRY

I don't seek attention to cry, instead to drive it right Strive
to make my society understand both sites We are al human
but mental y humorous I hope you wil process every "
kumaro"

I'm going deep to touch the history To tel you the stories
that are mysterious A good man can't be known by the face
Or how many good clothes he has worn Instead the faith
has a role to play Do your necessary exfoliate edition This
is not about a substitution process An eternal life forever is
the mission Likewise a good woman can't be defined by
the shape

But the heart would speak volumes about her taste We are
al learning after so many mistakes.

82

35. HOLD MY SOUL

Hold my soul cold

I'm not casting to surrender

74

Looking at you like my "Corriander"

You're my Indian resonance flavour Hold my soul cold

Allow not to be told

Shakespeare riding on my mind The love for turmeric lingering ginger Hold my soul cold

Configuring memories

Questioning where his heart belongs Hope I'm that close, to toast with your host I'm generated to take this oath The referee blowing the whistle foe Pitching over from the coach

I'm tasked to take this bow

He's like ' Wil you marry me?'

The poet replying!

Hold my soul cold.

83

36. COME BACK AROUND

Come back around, when love whispers To my soul I give a rest, dress to see the guest Place a cup of tea on the desk Swimming in a pool of mess

Stretch my neck to the east and west Longing for love

My heart screaming his lungs out Not a soul listens or hears me out My emptiness seems unbearable and My tastes seem unquenchable

Yet I'm in an abundance of water Again stuck in the fame of love To a world full of threats

I place my heart of trust

Cross you with al sorts of thoughts Corrupting thoughts of snatching love But patience holds me back

Knowing that the real love is yet to come around The paradox of finding Miss Right, Mr Right Overweighs the reality

84

SAFFIATOU JOOF

My imagination brings me to climax The feeling ceases to end

I wonder if I could just settle with that energy Not knowing that the actuality wil be as pleasurable What a love that I hang with faith and wish to see it around again

All the retirement of the long sweaty day It's going to be fine, welcome love again My energy rejuvenates, like it has never been gone Love please come back around

When shal I see you one more time?

Incredulously got gazes, beautiful in short days Strawberries clinging around

Sound of you touches the ground Orchestrates our love nest so soothing So calm and peaceful

The nights cease to end

Growing bigger and getting better Stretching further and further The bitterness of love was found My heart is not a rock

It was stuck, bul y of trust

85

UNDER THE SPELL OF POETRY

When wil love come back around?

When I shal smile one more time?

If love gives us another chance I promise to love me and you

I wil spend my lifetime with you Love, please come back around For I have missed those days surround.

86

37. HAPPY INTERNATIONAL WOMEN'S DAY

No woman no cry

No sweet honey from my mouth

No dear tears from my eyes

Teach a woman how to write

She would plant her tree with pride Even in the burning issues of crime Her voice would echo nothing to fright Solving her problems seven feet deep Singing the profound prose of Power Clutching the strings of her *kora* Changing the world within an hour The human heart with knowledge Contributing immensely to her children

'Making hay while the sun shines'

No woman no cry

No sweet honey from my mouth

No dear tears from my eyes

Our pronounced promised land of heaven Taking her lead without any grains That no coward man can stand her strength 87

UNDER THE SPELL OF POETRY

Her strength is a glowing wind of air Buried in her breastfeeding veins Succulent to her own sweats of oath The gifted patriotic woman

Trustworthy in her school of justice In the Quran she is told

Her inheritance she solely owns Her rights to speak her heart's opinion To pray and praise and choose For her business in my Jembe tone

"Na Koora Juloo"

"Na musu fingo, na musu koyoo"

No woman no cry

No sweet honey from my mouth

No dear tears from my eyes

Chanting the liberation of women We are born to rise and shine.

38. THE QUESTION ON AFRICA'S FREEDOM

I asked my mother, while in the kitchen seasoning the
chickens

Mum, when shal we be freed?

When shal I breathe the New Africa that we were
promised?

To grow our own rice fields

Brain crammed with new ideas

Empowered by the government

Led and executed in Africa

When shal we be freed?

That every child of a black mother Would have access to
education but free Water and electricity to be instal ed in
the whole nation

Our cultural norms would be valued and Businesses from
Africa would be respected In contact with my mother's
eyes Biting my lips, then Mum sneezed Her voice sounded
hopeless

Her body language was absent

"Very soon my baby girl, very soon"

UNDER THE SPELL OF POETRY

I imagine "The African story is bitter to swal ow"

I stood behind the door to speak I came here not to rest, but to rebuild that lost spirit That myopic mind is in prison, I'm not retiring and I won't resist

Rushing out from the kitchen

I vomited Africa; I think we are with a disease That needs our children to understand What is made in Africa?

What is empowering your mind?

Bring back the lost glory

Shouting loudly to the world

A nation of good faith but bad breaths (Governments)

Polluted Africa with corruptions Our youths become chronicles of no choice But join me; my spirit is here for a change My fight to ending mental slavery in Africa 90

39. INVISIBLE PARTNER

Tal soul, pointed nose, glittering lips and Fairy dark complex skin in the middle of the sunlight Breaded shrimps of smiles flustered in his eyes from the distance

The ghost of my heart

Flying with the early morning bird Your touch I grace

Thus a gifted hand so soft like grapes Your knowledge deeply amazes

When I'm lost, you clearly explain Your friendship quickly grows deeper flourishing like a flower

The only known tower whom I'm glued to his hours For
the Lord I pray you shal never negate Shift and suffer like a
pirate Your voice alone is strength

Born to train, rain and change I never predicted your star

But I feel that you're not far Even in the depth of the ocean
91

UNDER THE SPELL OF POETRY

I can't wait to see you surface by the hour But I know that
you are far away But very close to my palm.

92

40. TO YOU MY LOVE

All fades away in cast

All the nice time

Chats al fades away in fright Even the little smile

Fast too quick to shine

All fades away too fast

Ruffle the love of agony

Leakage of words stained

Not real from the tongue

Neither the heart pains

Non-patience too young for the games My love is blind to
see

Seek the course of the rigged Our hearts are cream with cheese Love climbed the ladder to scream Fake expressions covered with faith affection Mistakes blended with crispy attitudes Little issue makes it surge and trimmed Crime scenes are being seen

Hidden grudges are beneath

93

UNDER THE SPELL OF POETRY

Positivity sang arrogance

Tribune to the dying love

All fades away too fast.

94

41. TYRANT LEADERS

Man up, respect the voice of the people Ugandan hearts are full of pain Our world, with genuine flesh and blood is bleeding You're a coward

Hiding under the umbrel a of fear And advocating to Ugandans about care Silencing people do not dare

Be prepared to make a farewel here Thousands are out with Bobi Wine feathers That your men can't kil and clear Because freedom is blowing in the air For a day wil come, we wil share Our sleeping would be in our houses And yours would be in prison

You're manipulative, heartless and cruel Power hunger is foreseeable on your face Polling through the roofs of people The clock is the thickest bone, We're waiting patiently to reach the hour Your mind is currently freezing

95

UNDER THE SPELL OF POETRY

Uganda is far and near

To eternal source of freedom

Your regime is already crippling Your nights are getting darkened Neither the rain nor the storm celebrates you Your dreams are on the street dangling Nightmare is keeping you hanging Your biggest tree is bending

Your deeds have been covered

Your words have been slaughtered Your strength has been murdered And your time is being numbered We wil shoot combat your hurricane We're people other than dust

Within seconds we wil spread And shame you in tears

"People Power Our Power". Bobi Wine.

MY HEART BLEEDS FOR UGANDA.

96

42. ISLAM OUR MISSION

We are Muslim men and women full of good vision Islam is our life mission

Let us work towards a common solution And dispel our hearts from al il suspicions Our mission is not about division Our philosophy is al about divine submission To the will of Allah, the Eternal and Absolute Working for the

interests of Islam and al Muslims Together in solidarity
and partnership with our Muslim women

Singing true songs of freedom, development and justice for
al

An organization that would participate To create an
affirmative atmosphere For women and girls and students'
affairs Let us seek for reasons to heal And create a peaceful
environment for al tribes to speak

And fuel not our generation with fire and hate For our goal
is to take everyone into the highest heights

97

UNDER THE SPELL OF POETRY

We are here to create that care For our country we shal
cherish to share Working for numerous benefits That
would spark our country with bountiful treasures

That would stand for you when you're oppressed That shal
come with great national development projects

Nurturing our generations for many years with sustainable
success

Together, we as Muslims, are bigger and better!

98

43. HMD CHARITY FOUNDATION

HMD I trust in helping the needy people A non-
governmental organization Running and changing the life
of people Every vil age they target to make a difference
Every month they feed the most vulnerable families Your

84

donation wil only make them grow bigger It's not for fame, personal gain, or money It's just to lend a helping hand Something that you would be rewarded for And can't buy with wealth

Be part of changing the life of people From far and near

Be part of making the community better Than where they live

Non profit heroes

Automatical y making history

You can volunteer too.

99

44. WHY WE PRAY

With prayers many things can come from darkness into light

Anything hidden would come to surface It's a medicine to the heart, an exercise to the limbs A protection for the human being from al sorts of danger

It's healing and seasoning to the mind, pray That removes the heart from prison, pray We can't stop bleaching our skin, pray We can't stop drinking alcohol, pray And we can't stop wearing wigs or hair extensions, pray

Let's pray and ask Allah to remove our worst desires of life

Let's pray to make us believe in ourselves Trust Him; He would surface us as we pray Let's say, we do abuse our families Let's say, we don't want to take responsibilities

We are lazy and our hearts are hard-hearted Let's say, we
are women that don't cooperate with our husbands

100

SAFFIATOU JOOF

And want to be feminists at al times that lack the true
understanding of our religion Let's say, we are corrupt
individuals, and we can't be truthful for a second

Pray for Allah to show us the right path Whenever you're
lonely or feeling rejected, be little, worried

Confuse or facing financial problems, pray!

Because Allah won't leave you alone in your situations

Improvement of behaviour, character or attitudinal
problems, pray!

Anger management problem, pray!

This is the solution for every drop of tears For every heart
that is feeling pain For every door that seems hard to open,
pray May Allah bless us to get used to praying and praying
on time.

101

45. WHY DO I HAVE TO LOOK WHITE?

When the black skin has its own beautiful melanin To
protect us from the sun burns The fact that we believe that
the white skin is more beautiful than the black skin is
mental slavery The camera plays the biggest role cal filters
The TV instructed you that you need to make it brighter

It's even difficult to recognize the friends that we know
online when we see them live Such a deceptive life

Do you real y need to brighten your skin?

This false declaration of skin lightening starts from the
mind.

Degree holders are even being brainwashed That they
cannot escape from this trap Wearing hair extensions and
wigs Let's check again the definition of knowledge Which
means light and power?

Then that should liberate you from any form of slavery and
blindness

Use your knowledge to beam light into the life of your fel
ow sisters

102

SAFFIATOU JOOF

Arms and face completely different like Mars and Jupiter

Bleaching, toning, lightening and brightening have no
difference

Since they al have chemicals to alter the melanin Do you
real y need to brighten your skin or eat healthy foods?

For bleaching has so much pain The trading chain of skin
bleaching has changed Now parents are bleaching the skin
of their young children

Bleaching is very irritating and corrosive to the skin, lungs,
and eyes

Also, it has been known to destroy human tissues On top of
this, it may cause skin rashes and extreme headaches

A home full of bleaching humans That no silver or gold
could be achieved?

The dressing table arranged with bleaching products in a
row

Ready to flow, the scent seems so raw Even to the cold, in
this dust so rough, our women struggling to hold

103

UNDER THE SPELL OF POETRY

Even the environment has rejected skin bleaching Why do
I have to look white?

Let me breathe and let my thoughts run free Stil there's a
chance to rebuild that lost skin!

Deprived of natural colour

Free at last from slavery

Also it means to be free from skin bleaching.

104

46. THE BEGGAR

Body size so slime non good drink Get up early in the
morning in plain sleeves Without any food but hopes with
good dreams Leaning on his wheelchair

With the broken bowl, an unwanted cup, struggling to
count his fingers

People don't know how we feel We live a life that is so much hidden He grips, talking to his soul Begging the community, "I'm hungry"

Looking into the sunrise, with some prayers And sing it loud with a nice tune, 'I'm hungry"

"A beggar has no job but has strong faith in God Do remember them in their strange life That only few consider their existence But hopeful for the bowl

To be fil ed with some grains every day.

105

47. THE HAND THAT HOLDS ME

In the jungle of choices

You insist and cross.

In a caravan of war, shooting them al Leading me in a world of just Baby hold me, my emotions make it clear How much you mean to me while I wait to share I listen to your heartbeat in rhythm with my own With every pound that warming sound keeps me safe

With love you've shown

You brought me laughter, when I only saw pain Your hands so soft but strong You wrap me into your life

Put me where I belong

You hold me close and comfort me al Walk with me in the town like *King kong* Grateful forever I shal be in our kingdom.

48. THE DEPTH OF MY THOUGHT

Africa was brainwashed by France Invaded and made us become enemies And tactical y removed that attitude of sharing Trust was thrown into the bush Corruption becomes our societal pride Taking anything that they want from Africa Britain was the principal slaving nation of the modern world

The real debt is incalculable And they want me to become silent Silence for what would take us even more steps back No matter how many roads, schools and hospitals it built on the continent

And how much it has contributed to African economy

In the eyes of many observers, China cannot do 107

UNDER THE SPELL OF POETRY

nothing right in Africa

What have they changed in Africa?

For without Africa the modern world as we know it would not exist

Tel my children we need a solution Taking more debt is a civilized way of scolding us.

108

49. THE RADICAL FEMINISTS

Men our shades

Men our heroes

Get to the lake with the bait Refurbished the future with a
strong faith Do not accept a movement that is detrimental
to your taste

I am sorry

And be not like a lady

Who breaks into untwisted strands?

A faculty of young women

Spreading mischief to tear our men down Remember Allah
sets forth a parable A city enjoying nation

Abundantly supplied with sustenance Islam says justice,
not equal rights These are among the signs at the end of
time I grave, I terrace

I investigate

Out of the forest

I rise with my voice

109

UNDER THE SPELL OF POETRY

My heart is bleeding

The radical feminists come to lead Darkness covering their
eyes

Mental y enslaved

Veil under a movement

Ruling for equal rights with men Believing that being a single mother Forever is a pride

But the price is the menopause stage of complications and complaints

This wil lead them into the poolside of regrets Feminism official gender ideology Research results

Masquerades as a movement of women's rights In reality, feminism is a cruel hoax Tel ing women their natural biological instincts Are "social y constructed" to oppress them Feminism is elite social engineering Designed to destroy gender identity By making women masculine and men feminine Increasingly heterosexuals are conditioned To behave like homosexuals who general y don't 110

SAFFIATOU JOOF

marry and have children

To poison male-female relations (divide and conquer)

Their twin objectives are depopulation and totalitarian world government How many of our feminist marriages that are not at stake

Living a life that is fake

Modern feminism is a scam

Not in harmony with the teaching of Islam.

111

UNDER THE SPELL OF POETRY

50. THE MASS CHANGES

Scattered shal the stars be

Cleft asunder shal the heaven be Bursts shal the sea be

Upside down shal the graves be Vomiting out al their
content Round and its light is lost shal the sun be Pass
away the mountains shal be Pregnant she-camels neglected
shal they be Wild beasts gathered together shal be Man wil
be question about his sins Revealing pages of good and bad
deeds Good or evil persons shal be known Allah swearing
by the planets That disappear during the day And appear
during the night

Obedience is the angels to Him (Allah) But mans little
knowledge perceive not gays and lesbians choose not to
multiply But forgotten that they wil return to their Lord
Man looks at his good food

112

SAFFIATOU JOOF

But nay turns to be fooled

Water in abundance, olives and datepalms Gardens dense
with many trees And man stil questioning Who is God?

Have we forgotten how He (Allah) describes Hel fire?

To be in full view for everyone who sees Neither taste
therein nor any cool drink that hel shal be

But man's desires gripped him in lusts Hailing Paradise for
the people of good deeds Young full-breasted maidens of
equal age And a full cup of wine shal be Neither dirty,

93

false and evil talk nor lying shal be The lord of the heavens and the Earth And whosoever is between them, the most Gracious With whom they cannot dare to speak on the day of Resurrection

Except by His leave

Stand forth in rows the angels shal they be None speaks except him,

whom the most Gracious (Allah) al ows 113

UNDER THE SPELL OF POETRY

And He wil speak what is right The true day without doubt

So seek a place before dawn

A near torment we have been warned Don't wait until we wish to be dust.

114

51. AFRICA

Africa has been captured and captivated And my soul is crying,

As I am typing in a language, which is not mine What is wrong with our local languages?

I have lost the taste of my mother tongue I have been taught in a language That I struggle to learn

And put me into a system of education that wil cause delay to my future

A system of education that was built only to serve The interest of my slave master Believing in myself not any more The future of my generation wil be paying a bond That they don't seem to benefit from My culture and traditions have been belittled And my people have built up so much hatred to each other

That they don't celebrate one another A single soul came and played their tactics And won the battle so easily

That my children's eyes are blindly accepting 115

everything out of nothing

They said we cannot do anything to ourselves And that we are not even capable I am stabbing, pinching my body out of respect Because everything about my children's life was borrowed

Our originality, our mentality and the spirits that embody Africa are weak

And the Jinns that possess

Her children are indeed sick

You have to first slap Africa In order for it to understand that This system is not designed to be Africans She needs to be its own engineer, astronaut, doctor, and agricultural specialists

In order to cure its children from this il ness We have to fal in love with ourselves again Sometimes I feel like not saying a word I want to go back to that generation of ancient Egypt.

116

Where civilization began

That chapter of Africa begging has to end And open a new
page for our country.

117

52. HUMANKIND

Amazing that Allah has created Humankind with simple
clay

Looking at the beautiful waves of the ocean That don't
have any branches

The sea breeze that is mind-blowing Compared to nothing
on earth

Covering al the living things inside it That can't be seen
without diving into the ocean How magnificent that Allah
has been Looking into the skyline

That beautiful moonlight that smiles at you These
wonderful and pure white clouds That fashion without fal
ing down Those planets that line up with mil ions of miles
and they wil never meet

The ability to talk without much energy The energy to
learn with wisdom That wisdom to teach and sort out our
differences The ever-green trees that surround the earth
And the plant that you seeded 118

SAFFIATOU JOOF

And it grows overnight

The birds that fly without any effort of humankind How dare we question the existence of Allah?

119

53. RAMADAN

Some cal it Ramazan

Some cal it Ramadan

The ninth most blessed month of Islam It's the fourth pil ar of Islam It's a month to commemorate the first revelation of the Al' Quran

To Muhammad Salal ahu Alaihi wa Salaam I cal it Ramadan

Laylat al Qadr "The night of power"

Which the holy knowledge was gifted to Muhammad Salal ahu Alaihi wa salaam

So be prepared to perform the nightly prayers, including the obligatory prayers Let us take this chance

To become conscious of our creator Let's cease this chance

Increasing our awareness of His Majesty Exalting and glorifying His names Appreciating His greatness

120

SAFFIATOU JOOF

Recal ing His blessings upon us And being grateful and thankful for His guidance From the Quran Allah states

97

'O you who believe, fasting is prescribed for you As it was prescribed for those before you So you may remain conscious of Allah"

Ramadan comes to develop and strengthen our powers of self-control

Refraining from natural human urges, lusts and desires

Exercising our ability of self-restraint And apply it to our everyday life To bring about self-improvement I cal it Ramadan

Usual y the meal is simple

Designed to provide nourishment Usual y charity is given

And generosity is urged

We learn to give and not to take 121

UNDER THE SPELL OF POETRY

To remind us the less fortunate, the poor and the destitute

That contribute to the purification of our hearts and tongues

By cutting ourselves from worldly comforts At the end of this blessed month Eid al Fitr

The time of giving gifts

Sharing foods, gathering with family and friends When I think of Ramadan

I'm in a haste to get in touch With that holy blessed month of Islam.

54. MY WOMAN

Being the most wretched girl

That has no moral traits

Immodesty and insolence don't mean that you're intel igent

Being the most expensive, aggressive girl in that
neighbourhood

Who doesn't have any respect for herself Stepping
everywhere

Talking everywhere

Doesn't mean that you're smart Being that cheap girl

Who is answerable to every tick and tack of their cal
Doesn't symbolize that you're the identity card of his heart

Neither the scent of their fragrance burns through their skin
like sunrays

Nor his shining and glittering diamond of his choice Their
choice isn't that girl full of swag Their choice isn't that hot
girl full of attitudes The way we choose our foods wisely
that's the same way that men choose their spouses 123

UNDER THE SPELL OF POETRY

Girl, open up your eyes and be wise Because intel igence is
based on respecting yourself Allowing your parents to
control you Listening to advice, choosing the rightful
friends Lowering down your wings and feel that you're just
a human being on this earth

And not above the sky

As an intel igent woman

Her smile shines beautifully

Like the sun rising over the horizon She is the genuinely
caring woman Who goes the extra mile to help one in need
Just to make everyone smile

Even the love and happiness one inspires

She is a woman that one can count on And her knowledge
permits you to see when you're in darkness

She doesn't jump into conclusion Instead draws up
solutions

And her intel igence, wisdom and hard work in her married
life,

124

SAFFIATOU JOOF

Is not a battlefield because she is a wife that has patience

To correct things in her life Girl, embrace your religion and
respect your education

And you wil attain self-knowledge.

Enrich your mind with positive thoughts, And stop the
manipulation of this physical or material world.

As intel igent women

We must address ourselves to several critical questions

The answer to these questions Wil guide our search both
for content and methodology

For we are women that are mental y, physical y, social y,
political y

And psychological y potential Let's use our intel igence
wisely.

125

55. A MESSAGE TO THE GOVERNMENT

There is a trust that Allah has given us There is a trust that
our wives have given us There is a trust that our parents
have given us But the greatest is your nation And you need
to fulfil that trust I simply ask the government of The
Gambia What have you planned for the needy people?

Where has the money been used?

People that live from hand to mouth The handicaps, the
blind people, and the disabled people

That their shoulder be touched But have you declared a
constant food supply?

How many people wil stay a day without having food on
the table?

Wil our government surrender their lives to them?

Mr. President

You're being served constantly with food But someone is
crying out there without food You don't make
manifestations When it comes to the situation 126

101

And how wil people be helped?

Gambian people entrusted you

Remember that you wil be questioned about your nation

And when Allah bestowed upon you this great nation

What efforts have you made to put a smile on the people's
face?

For the grace is not only for you But always remember to
uphold our hearts. .

127

56. I AM CORONA VIRUS

Not datepalms with soft spandex Not mountain houses with
great skil s Not the command of the people Can cage me
like generics

My release was a metric spreading like euphoric I came to
the world al of a sudden while they perceived it not

I take control of the roads, mosques and close down
businesses

I don't look at your wealth or the amount of poverty that
you possess

And touch me not with hands, but to keep a distance I'm
merely corona, making corruption, deaths and mischief in
the lands

As I got registered, my legacy began to mark the traits

And I won't be convicted neither jailed nor declared for
war

128

SAFFIATOU JOOF

The day of shadows has ceased Human beings denying me
to take a seat I am the king of the land

In every land of media I lead Pandemic I was cal ed but
many have forgotten the renewal of faith

A farewel good of taste

My virus cannot be caged

And touch me not with hands, but to keep a distance
Indeed this is a sign, yet most of them do not believe Never
did I destroy a township without bringing warnings

In the land that you breathe

Being taught the language of birds But give an ear to the
devils In the land that you and I have sins Obeying the
superpowers

Not remembering feeding the poor Fornication becomes a
source

Corona is a burning brand that you may warn 129

UNDER THE SPELL OF POETRY

yourselves.

And glorified is Allah, the Lord of the Alamin.

"La ilaha il ahuwa"

The son of Adam is weak.

The daughter of Awa is creep.

Desperate in need of seed to keep corona at sleep, The community looks dry, the economy is dying.

The children rise but the adults die.

The nation tries, the society cries.

Our doctors fight but the corona is tight.

We lost some loved ones, our friends and the like.

Pray to your lord, please stay at home.

Spiritual fight and emotional fight won't drive corona away.

Wash your hands, cover your mouth and do your repentance.

I am corona and my vaccine is to keep a distance.

(I AM CORONA VIRUS, THIS IS AMONG THE BEST

POEMS OF EU AT THE TIME OF THE PANDEMIC 2019) 130

57. THE USE OF BAD LANGUAGE (INSULTS)

It must be said

When you are too arrogant

You can easily be possessed

Why being obsessed and upset?

Its truth that goes direct into the heart Humankind sometimes is too comfortable breathing freely

And thought that free words are a pride to voice When invested in pain or feel that it's been defeated Knowledge isn't like anyone and doesn't require us to acquire it forcefully

Knowledge is wise, and Allah grants it to anyone that He wishes

Knowledge is wisdom; it takes one from darkness to light

A smal child can drink from the vessels of the elders If that child has discipline and being obedient to ALLAH

Our parents seeded this generation and we are yet to harvest

131

UNDER THE SPELL OF POETRY

That is why we should choose our words wisely True knowledge is hidden, it is only being noticed when voice out

Only a rude parent that was brought up insolently Would have dirty words to voiced It is such parents that have accommodated SHAITAN

into their houses

That shows within their speeches and attitudes Once you insult someone through briefing or introduction of any statements Allah has taken away its blessings I observed many youths like getting into the shoes I question whether it's from the homes Ways of silencing people or it is just a culture It's a shame on our generation of bachelor's, master's and PhD degrees

That is stil behaving like a toddler Do we want to be stil reminded that we are no more in primary schools?

I mean grow up

I mean desist from it

132

SAFFIATOU JOOF

And I mean you surpass that stage I mean we are not in the warfield I mean we are brothers and sisters of this nation If insulting people could have been a culture We wil not have The River Gambia That flows from the *FOUTA JALON* highlands The sunbird doesn't hate the hawk, so why us?

This is someone's father, mother, sister and brother Let's behave like the mangroves in the swamps That are rapidly growing to protect the river We have the most navigable river Let's be like the transnational function of Barra and Banjul

Farafenni and Yelitenda

The Gambia is a centre

Think about it when you are about to insult your brothers.

58. MUNYAL (BE PATIENT)

After she was beaten baselessly And aimlessly he awakens her to complete his night duties

The elders of the community wil encourage her to be patient

After she was abused over many times After giving her names

She won't ever produce a productive child Her problem was the topic in town Give her names that she doesn't even deserve That your fel ow women are going through that And that nobody heard them talking about it

"Munyal" becomes a ring tone of the tongue That gave privileges to some men to open their mouths

That some wil continue to abuse our young vulnerable women

"Sey moo ko waral"

134

SAFFIATOU JOOF

You didn't have the sympathy, why making her cry?

Sad that our women are traped into a can of belief When Islam has given her the right to speak We don't want to lead, but some are bleeding Our fel ow women are suffering in the hands of some men

I tel you, don't forget your rights You have rights over him
before the sunrise Because clothing, feeding and shelter are
part of his right

You have right over him before the sunset Before marrying
a second wife, he has to be in full set

The Sunnah isn't half, practise the full set Secrecy goes
with saving your dignity and integrity Real men don't beat,
don't fight and shout on women.

135

59. JEALOUSY

Hold your breath

A jealous heart wil never rest in peace Perhaps we're not
from the same breed And the "deen" didn't teach us to be
greedy This "dunya" is not a weed as it is seen So
everything you seed, you wil of course reap Listen to me
deep

Jealous of what?

Is it the worldly life, the titles or position That we wil die
and leave

Remember you're each other's keeper Meeting when we
feel a need

But jealousy separated our paths Don't we feel ashamed to
look at someone's face That we had already slandered
These words are hard to swal ow It's like eating someone
flesh Listen to them as they mouth your name They talk of
your ways, following up your successful days

SAFFIATOU JOOF

Creating a scene, even if you're not on stage Believers whose words describe nothing but misery Hearts start beating rapidly, lungs oxygenating quickly

Leaving nothing, instead of jealousy Is this the life we want to live?

Tarnishing each other like we don't have a "deen"

Don't forget your own deeds

Don't smile at him when you know that it's not mean

Jealousy composers have no more creativity Their happiness al is in agony So feed their eyes continuously And live your life happily

A jealous heart wil never rest in peace.

60. LOVE RESIDES

The place where love recites

To many, they got the meaning but precised Some thought that it is the body size The facial beauty, the shape and the like But the deen actual y decides When true love stands stil and recites It is normal

When hypocrites hope like they want to take a flight Testifying your true love is not an act of worship But stay in the residence of secrecy Governed by people of dignity, handled by people of personality

Take bath in the pool of love, to al seasons, and reasons

And love to eternity.

138

61. WOMAN OF MY HEART

The twinkle star

How I wonder what you are

Looking into the sky feeling so sad Don't be scared,
you've got my back This bond is so tight

That it can't be separated so fast You are my star

I'm the sticker that wil stick to your back Like the butterfly
that greets you every night You're my honey, the taste of
my tea The commander in charge of my house You are my
woman without being mad Why thinking otherwise?

Dear favourite lovely wife.

You cooked the dinner so nice 139

UNDER THE SPELL OF POETRY

And served it so wise

With my favourite juice

I have no comment

If you cook the rice so bad

I wil never take it so hard

I have no comment

If you behave like a child

Remember

You're the mother of my children You're the twinkle star

That always melts my heart

Oh! Dear woman of my life.

140

62. THE MONTH OF RAMADAN

It is a month of obligation

Dominating the whole nation

This is total liberation

Some love it, cal ing it the month of civilization An act of goodness wil serve as remuneration Let's commemorate the night of declaration Let's accelerate the celebration The purpose of the Quran is to educate the generation

To avoid temptation

Read, listen and obey the book of revelation Don't neglect the opportunities granted in this powerful month of consideration Amplifying our purification

Increasing our connection

And decreasing our love for this world of deception What a big preparation

That every Muslim wil be in a state of expedition To be in
touch with this sacred month of Ramadan 141

UNDER THE SPELL OF POETRY

Stop listening to my redeem of redemption And listen to
the words of reflection Seizing our soul from defamation
Just like the waves of the ocean Oh Allah wipes out our
sins

So that we won't sink

Give us strength to be king

And reap the pleasure it brings And renew our vision and
restrain us from division This is not hal ucination

I kept it from the root, my heart of edition So recite the
Quran, with a stoical voice of concern Give charity to the
destitute You're building your own institute Hold tight to
your Quran

Read the Sourat Al-Furqan

If you have gone to a stage of depression Open your Quran,
and you wil see the solution.

142

63. MY GAMBIA

What kind of time are these

Where our norms and values are forgotten That a hard-
working person want to be lazy Unity is not a song in our
vil ages How sweet our nation would have been If
forgotten feelings were rekindled anew If power could
have been like a drink That every family would fetch its

own tanker To have equal right and quick dispensation of justice It is not the most satisfying for the soul It is not the wish to keep hidden in my breast What kind of times are these?

In a land where power is weak In a land where knowledgeable people are becoming limited

In a land where tribalism is beginning to have a place to breathe and breed

143

UNDER THE SPELL OF POETRY

In a land where political misunderstanding influences hatred

Where is love for mother Gambia?

144

64. CONVERSATION WITH LOVE

Love cal my NAME

And I wil answer within my GATE

Love take my HEART

And I wil give it out with GRACE

Love knock at my door and I shal show you what it TAKES

Love CALL me into a COURTHOUSE

And I wil wil ingly take that OATH

Love dispel al my DOUBTS

And I wil remove al the FEARS

Love GROW into my heart

And I wil give out the chance to share Love SIT in my
heart

And I wil NURTURE you with care Love glance at me and
I wil open my heart to STORE

it

Listen to me and I wil give you Mandela's wisdom It's a
quiet SENSATION don't confuse it with INFATUATION

It's a sealed PACKAGE

145

UNDER THE SPELL OF POETRY

Which only comes with PATIENCE

So when they chorus it in HASTE

You take it with FAITH

The meaning of love aims at ETERNITY

Protecting you with its cloak of SECURITY

Pure love gives you PEACE

And SURPASSES al these dreams Pure love destroys
CAGES and brings feelings into REALITY

Pure love wails and cures al SICKNESSES

SUCCESS hailing ordering al birds to SING your NAME

Shaitan is easily detected

When love outcasts al your SINS

Enemies fearing that love wil give you hope of many dreams

Singing your NAME

And love replied not with PAIN

Keep your head STRAIGHT; you didn't build love in a TRAIN

146

SAFFIATOU JOOF

Close your EYES and EARS

Love concords al these GAMES

Love for the sake of Allah is one of the strongest bonds of faith

And the most important foundation on which Muslim society is based

It is the basis by means of which ties of friendship And harmony among people are attained So that they may love one another But our generation needs to be sensitized Love commanded them to behave.

147

65. THE UPRISING WOMAN

She has risen from her own seat Smiles to show out her
euphemism teeth Then my heart beats, wisdom she speaks
She is reasoning how too much to give The physical beauty
she manifested truly set her free Of course, nobody can
cage her tree It's bound to grow up to her feet Her spirit
now heightened, she feels angry But looks at everything
greatly Majestical y, she walks spiritual y The redeem of
her voice echoe through the mike Energetical y, yet firmly,
confidence she greets

"I am a woman"

Mistakenly, some never understood That a woman is an
added value in any man's dream Even Allah gave us our
own rights But as we try to capture the world Enemies and
rapists hoping to take advantage 148

SAFFIATOU JOOF

Remember, I kick away pride, I stop sparkling tears I
swore an oath, so please help me God It is the way I
believe, not the way you believe Many stil have tried to
find out in their own means When they try to read us, what
is in us?

Together, that strength of our souls Our spirits and our
powers are going to be seen Maybe the bounce of our
breasts, makes them blind Maybe the coolness of our eyes
makes them lust Maybe the curves of our bodies that's why
some thought that we're weak

Respect we need just like the sunshine Protection we need
just like the hopes springing But don't ever dream that we'l
bow down our heads and lower our eyes;

The creation of our body was not made for enslavement.

We wil rise up!

149

66. IT IS SPREADING LIKE AN INFECTION

It is spreading like an infection Almost in every corner of
the country The channels that we use to fight for corruption
Is it controlled by the people who actual y fight against
corruption?

They only talk with an action When there is public reaction
I'm sad because it is now a profession Hailed by the mafia,
wailed by the poor people Addressing across the whole
nation Leaders are supposed not to take it as a word of
connotation

These are serious matters that need immediate
consideration

Let us stop making commotion and apply measures Our
voices are not heard like we have no choice I'm
flabbergasted because our country is being raped.

150

67. RESPECT HER NO

Some women are being molested Subdued to an action that
has to be unveiled But yet we can't name their names; but
can number their dates

They're not lovers

A lover is one who waits

Who won't force for a date

But you stop her from achieving her dreams What a pain in her heart, stil unhealed Our lives that we live are created by our lord Remember, woman

You were born, fearless and sweet You were born with wisdom and sealed Passion to name your own destiny Be like an arrow

Your mountain is unshakable

You have the infinite key letters to your door So to none should you kneel

151

UNDER THE SPELL OF POETRY

Upfront, rooted in pain,

Let's respect her No!

152

68. TYRONE ALLEYNE

I learnt how to play chess

At an age that I believe it was a test Portraying poetry as an access The farm I needed to seed

I remember, his name is TM

He plays poetry with confidence That teaches me no rules

But believes that my talent was a screw Not like a lost child

That I found him as a clue, glued to his shoes I can't be anything without his school; 153

UNDER THE SPELL OF POETRY

He has shown me the roads

The dots the angle of my path And given me not false hope

Taking me into a land where glitters are formed
Connecting me to the corridors of this world And today I
can shine longer with his hat on I was afraid that one day, I
wouldn't find him And tel him how I have been
transformed But grateful

I shal cherish this gift, being forever in his club Giving him
a cal is the strongest thought that I know It's a remarkable
moment, in my household That today, he's reading the
discovered chess of his student.

154

69. OUR RELIGION

Our faith can't be chained or got stuck in one place Our
religion is unpaid from Allah we expect rewards 570 AD, a
prophet was born, even the *JINNS* were afraid

A religion was introduced and Islam was its name Allow
the peace to prevail, we have been guided to the straight
path

All the idols were destroyed

Name; of course Muhammad was his name Even Jesus
(Essa) confessed, manifested and describe his faith

He's kindness, loyalty and honesty, oh the last Prophet of
Allah

ABDULLAH was his father and AMINA was his mother

He was a man unable to read or write But when the
revelation came

That's when Gibril said,

"Read Muhammad, and Muhammad reads Read in the
name of your Lord who created"

155

UNDER THE SPELL OF POETRY

Adam was created without a mother and father Jesus (Essa)
was born with a mother and no father We human beings,
have a mother and father Truly these are among the signs
of the miracles of Allah.

Born in Mecca and migrated to Medina He preached to al
people to see that Islam prevailed He face many hardships,
many sufferings and trials Married to Khadijah, who was
named the mothers of the believers

Truly Muhammad, you're the messenger of Allah Since
1400 AD, this religion has never changed The gate of the
Prophethood has forever been closed

No doubt to his legacy,

He has been given the true revelation That the Ummah
should preach with its admonition Islam became unique,
only to worship One God.

156

70. TREMBLING

The clock is ticking

Looking into my eyes, I am scared Scared of whatever this truth shal be The fakeness bolded in our eyes The smile that was never real I feel like the heroine in a horror movie Gasping the handle, cal ed to different names This is the ghost of al hosts I am, I wil and I shal be

I am closing the chain of friendship in my life You just need a smal circle to sail Like a boat on the float

Apparently noteworthy to your talent Be your own engineer

Battling out your sorrows

There is a secret, without much condition To do what you can do.

157

71. IN MY WOMAN'S VOICE

Dear future husband

We are not a piece of cloth

Neither a piece of cotton

Nor some pieces of tissue paper That are supposed to be used

Anyhow, anywhere and anytime

Instead, we're a special package Sent to you (men) by Allah

We are more than gold and diamonds That died in every man's heart That could stil stand stil

And control the globe into our hands I wish she understands her powers What a captivating soul that SHE could be Yet to be respected and honoured I salute men that value us women Those who never raise a hand on us Perhaps understand the value of our existence.

158

72. THE CAST CALL

The dots you have to connect

Each stage has its own pain

Too afraid but you're not too late Difficulties you face to cross the bait Those lakes, rivers and oceans Full of sharks, whales and snakes All the dangerous animals surrounding you As your soul struggle hard to breathe Down on the narrow roads they want you to perish Encountering everything alone Wondering why it never went right Always know that you're not alone Because Almighty God controls everything The examination of the Earth

Beyond our knowledge memory card Our eyes cannot see

And our minds and intel igence cannot comprehend The coloration of nature

159

UNDER THE SPELL OF POETRY

That can never be fully described by any The vast energy of the wind

That has no limit that can be imagined The bil ions of secrets within the depth of the ocean That no scientist can

123

dive to see to finish The ocean which is an immensely abundant source of water

But a tanker has only a limited capacity to take from it

Looking at the morning sun bird That wil resist the gravity of the Earth and take a fly If truly your heart beats with the love of God And flows over with the belief In the creator of al beings

In the midst of the most complex difficulties We should never be discouraged And lonely but hopeful

That only Allah is the greatest.

160

73. AFRICA, OUR HOMELAND

Let's strive together to develop And promote our own projects

Unity is the backbone of progress and success The freedom

Which we have to cherish

And live with every day

If our faith and trust are in Allah Betrayals and disappointments Shouldn't be within us

Let's fight ignorance and start learning Giving chance to the less privileged Lets Love and stop tarnishing each other's image And improve under one umbrel a Our leaders should draw up solutions And fulfil their promises

Keep us, Great God

And protect our Africa every day.

161

74. THE BLACK WOMAN

Black, thick, hard

Having the colour of dark

Kind, walking through the darkness of the sun-shine

Too natural, reflecting the nature of the *Kaaba* Make her
your *Kabaa*

Te du foro tol, nekut borom hol Kom Hitler sohor' bon

My African queen, be my twin

With no wrinkles, shining like the twinkle star Too natural
and blowing like gas

"Bari Hel o, Mama Africa"

"Al a gel ow, melodious voice "

Rocks your bones like "cocktail"

Cal ing her "Nna gaalow"

Come and be my sparrow

You are my bone marrow

Because she is far from women of "fansorow"

162

SAFFIATOU JOOF

I am sorry,

But this is not a request; protect your black woman And kindly rest, and do your best Skin black, walk black and worn black Even the great Mandela had that been confessed

"Freedom cannot be achieved unless women have been emancipated

From al forms of suppression and oppression"

I am cal ing for liberation, dedication Operation respect to your education My heart got stuck, struck to the falsehood Shown to a black woman, that wasn't good Took the street school life at an early youth Common to be used as a tool

The aim to destroy our hood

"Al kaa kele"

Come to the mirror " nha fele "

Slow white horses fashions and announces The black woman

She is the reason industries invented lip gloss and lipstick

Her beauty is where love resides ready to fly 163

UNDER THE SPELL OF POETRY

You won't ever fully understand at night Her teeth shine like the shattered twinkle stars She is the only queen whose waist isn't round or oversized

164

75. DEAR SOLO SANDENG

I point a finger at your death For the longest history that
I kept in my heart I revisited, for The Gambia to
understand my quest Today I speak of how I felt

The last news of you being missing shocks Behold, my
hand on the cel phone and whisper Over the years I heard
of this trauma but insisted is he truly missing?

As the fatal news arose through the length and breadth of
this nation

Murmuring into the cabinet, what happened to democracy?

UNDER THE SPELL OF POETRY

A sacrifice you have made to sing the last words of
freedom

Shattered my heart remains stagnant, blown by the wind of
surprise

Disturbed at the missing news, followed by the sudden
death, it was a rumour As daylight increased and
decreased, the news became clear

It became a truth, a loss of appetite found me from school

For the longest history that I stil kept in my heart I point a
finger at your death For the inhuman display by the regime
Brutal y tortured, I heard they refused to let you breathe

To let you say one sentence of my freedom When the
TRRC emerged, its injury looked fresh Your quest to fight
for the freedom of democracy isn't just lip service

Your request for the interest of liberation isn't just a little
effort

Your braveness further blown our minds, that it's not just a
one party politics

But ending tyranny, injustice, disappearing 166

SAFFIATOU JOOF

kidnapped and detained

But ending fear, dictatorship, hunting of humans,and
perpetual y insecure

But ending the risk involves speaking To be conscious of
our rights in our nation I thank you for taking your stand to
see that I speak You have uprooted a dictator to grant your
children peace

Who alone controls our system and sterilizes the judiciary

And today we prevail with your flag of freedom The
missing bones we have found make us stronger Buried
your remains within the ears of thinkers Your justice is
grave and succulent to our oath Confirming to my freedom
of expression Paying my last respects to the battle to win I
continue to point a finger at your death Until the culprit is
brought to book for you to rest.

167

76. THE EMBLEM TO MY HEART

I cal the name of my queen

Pulling down everything within a blink My fingers are
level

Already honouring your ring

My twin, oh my king

Looking up into the sky for you to sing In my ears, I heard
the whistle From the distance of the kettle Meditated deep
into our chats And twisting the kora strings Because he is
snatching everything Your heartbeat I thought

Your words got an echo

None has it taken me to court So difficult for me to quote

But got me so much involved

77. UNDER OUR BEAUTIFUL TENT (GINA BASS)

Our gold winner, a chosen national gem Putting up an effort like a stem So witty to swing you with surprises That would grow to bear fruit In the middle of daylight then trends

"Gina Bass, Awo yaay Halam

Like Demba meyti wonna, dila gerrem"

Breaking records and crossing bridges By passing the beat breed of tal woods Surrender to the point of strength You sweat it further, jumps al 169

UNDER THE SPELL OF POETRY

"Ndakh danga nopi te nyemeh, hareng"

Who can be like her in the lane of gym?

Training regularly with a dream She worked it, sweated it and brought it home

"Dua nding mbaa jabitta" history was made The
motherland is feeling proud In the crowds of Konya
Olympic in Turkey Gina strongly got crowned

Glimpsing the beautiful face of her *tamanya* Got in return
fil ed up space of her *bori nya* Not slow like a lion running
for a feast But even cheese can't melt from such heat
Quick to realize that Gina has finished Giggled from the
smile of the teddy bears A prize you work with no petty
gear Oh Gambia, I cal for her decor Specialty in return for
her welfare Because Gina is a gem so rare to be seen
Uniting a whole nation like a queen Walking in the tower
to see the flower It's a breath taken on the map shining
Who dare doubt what Gina can bring.

170

78. CELEBRATING A LIVING LENGEND

HONOURABLE SIDIA JATTA

In early 1945, a legend was born Like a rainstorm from the sky That comes down as a gift to humankind A man of his words, who speaks truth without fear He never beats around the bush When it comes to the needful

A politician, he has been for ages But never shal he retire in our minds He fought for us as if it was mandatory With his work, no question or alteration 171

UNDER THE SPELL OF POETRY

A servant he has been to his people But the Gambians didn't see it earlier But just notice his strife as a socialist And some forgot to mention him as a hero Because the children of Adam

Understand less about his agenda But now the record is marking average I respect you for your sufficient knowledge I respect you for your untiring efforts None shal I dispute your integrity Because dignity exists in your spirit We have bitten our fingers upon hearing Purchased an error in exchange for good leadership That is a mistake of darkness, thunder, and lightning You have fuel ed a sincere knowledge towards the youths.

But not with stones of no weight in the air That we wil miss to see in the Parliament He fought corruption in the centre to correction Mosquito bites are always distractive But his party bites for sustainable generations That only a few understand those scriptures 172

Establish to place The Gambia on the map I wrote this poem deep to live up to eternity Even the devil can't stop this mainstream It's a love from the drops of the fountain Your legacy demonstrated a clear mountain That I wil revive perhaps of you humbly That I wil rewrite in the books of history That give me the confidence to script you gracefully.

173

79. DARK FEATHERS

Your feathers have touched my knees Your friends once Googled my name Your family once embraced me like a bird This gives me more time to believe you Convince me not based on your rings Neither the house you built

None on how much you fenced

But be fair to yourself, stop the sugar coating In my ears, you're promised and it sinks Don't be a chameleon so slow

Next to my elbow, you crawling judge Talk back to my back you laugh Just to check what's on my faith We dream as teenager they admire You crave the avenue of trust Broke the tedious times yet you lost Came into my life like a fresh apple Only to cut it and realize that it's rotten Turning back was too late for me Friends couldn't rescue, my feathers flew 174

SAFFIATOU JOOF

Flew to the atmosphere with my struggle He has come into my life for a reunion But now my eyes are plague open Stay away from my lane

Drain not these remains of human flesh Dark intentions eventual y get exploded.

80. RAMADAN KAREEM

On this auspicious day

On this very bonded day

That touched the life of every Muslim soul Clunge with hunger and minimum food Got us cool but with too much to learn Understand that God exists somewhere Somewhere with hopes to see His Prophet Embracing the most elegant Quran Detailing what life means to start on earth Lucky to be born a Muslim apart Upon our struggles, we stil have faith in Him alone A beginning voyage of such good deeds counts A lifetime excursion during Ramadan Better than the remaining months of al ure That brought our Imman close to our face Shaped our beliefs and regained our health For every laziness has purely been cured Ramadan fades away as our last day But the good it brought rebranded our faith For life seems temporal, God is a source 176

SAFFIATOU JOOF

Never forget to give Him his due As in our hearts, we are sending Ramadan Kareem God has truly touched and blessed our lives Grateful to witness this radiant beam Grateful to awake the spirit of love The Quran serves as a guide to humankind Would you read my sermon is a quest Being reasoning after just one season With our eyes to continuing this strong faith Be flourishing with magnificent strength We try to be truthful about al that blew Don't forget the orphans, as you were doing Our women in the kitchen shal be praised As the light stone is energetical y engaged Delivering the best meal in a timely fashion That tenses the stomach to eat healthily Bravo to the men, who fascinated their efforts Everyday fishing, none has broken the hearts To put a smile on the children's profile Thanks for giving and never complaining Thanks for sharing and never comparing Thanks for accepting and never looking dul 177

UNDER THE SPELL OF POETRY

The hil of this month might be tight As darkness at night, did not stop our *tahajud* May its blessings keep us steadfast.

178

81. RENEWAL

But never lose hope, our desires are high We asked for forgiveness from Allah To renew our faith

We pray for His mercy to the human race To grant Palestine peace from their oppressors To grant the world peace from wars and poverty To respect people and the elderly imams Their contribution this month should be news Renewal of our attitudes is a needed space To live a dignified life on the planet Earth To honour our parents for their endeavours To honour the truth as we engage in speech Humiliation never befal s our ceiling To protect our progeny from Shaitan I send you the message of peace.

179

82. NATIONAL ASSEMBLY MEMBERS

Within the hours of Fajir, I welcome the win Men and
women were final y chosen with a clause A dream to the
National Assembly got surplus As the surprising result
busted A foresight of tights wasn't seen Wails are heard
from people awake A sealed off the close-range goal
session Bal possession of limited defeats The halfway rule
of the government redeemed The halfway rule of the
opposition gears up The halfway rule of the independent
candidates pops

Battle of interest could be sensitive 180

SAFFIATOU JOOF

Rigid parliament is a means to breathe Hopes quarterly
prove but filth Voters build their dreams so soon Puddles
of warning rain in hips To sel not their party colours

sleeves But sel in the interest of the Gambian dreams
Loyalists warn MPs of the brown envelopes Stand not to
vote in sugarcoat laws Stand to fight for your community's
causes To remember the outcry of what poverty posts The
country's eyes are on you al Let actions speak louder than
words The overal Gambian interest first Our cultural sweat
must be a lead Don't make dirt on the cloth we give Let's
wait for history to rewrite your names Either among the
loyalists or The betrayal MPs of season.

181

83. TILAPIA FISH

I cal you to the good food

To make our stomach full

To the taste that we ever knock down to Before it wil serve
to cool

We did the suffering period to bait the fish One happy day,
on a Sunday

The selection was made for the best fish We were quick to
point out our possibilities The nation gathers to put their
efforts This big tilapia fish, in the sea, we catch together
With the bruises and threatened, yet we stay firm We
covered it and give the country hope Already being washed
clean to steam Retouch the tilapia fish with the gil s Throw
up some black paper on it Rub it with some mustard

Pound the garlic, give al necessary flavours As it makes
sense of the oil frying pan The man runs down with the
tilapia fish Then beg the fish to heal

182

I think it is sick, he starts the tricks Reddish-brown

He refused to move the fish in the nation's eyes Put on the gas for some temporal heat It's ready to serve with some onions He slices it into pieces

Instead of cal ing the nation to eat And ghetto it with the youths He settles alone with few to eat the nation's fish This is one of the tricks that politicians played on their patriotic citizens

Vote wisely and peacefully.

183

84. TAP WATER

When no one believes in your work When nobody thought that your tap water isn't fresh

Is not lucrative, or won't pay off When your close friends distance themselves When you were left with few souls to dine with When everything you could have ever wanted to be Shocked up blown, and become hopeless You look left and right

Come to understand that

That wasn't you

Redefine that part and hold on to your sight It's not them that can design your life It's you that can open that part It's you that know, how deep that wound looks Everything in the starting could be difficult It may be a waste of time

It seems that your colleagues have left you behind No, it's
your time that has not arrived It's not easy to catch a big
fish from the ocean It's not easy to fetch water from the tap
184

SAFFIATOU JOOF

Yes, it has to be fresh water So that everyone would drink

Including those that didn't believe in your part To drink
from your tap.

185

85. TOXIC RELATIONSHIPS

A toxic relationship is like a global pandemic It takes you
down to the gutter to drain you It's as beautiful at the
beginning as an art That minimizes within the limits of
emotion It's a usable road with an emotional symbol It's a
belittling control affectionate fighting That the partner
thought you are a perfectionist An infal ible spouse that
gives you little to cry A dominant that left you on planet
Earth Swindled your intel igence and silenced you The
insecurity is mind-blowing like termites That bite the smal
est space in your life The fear of being left alone in control
of sights There is no one like him or her as enormous By
always taking a lead and not being faulty Your ideas are
Skype to kil that energy in you Hitler in disguise, nobody
chal enges decisions They trouble you today, massage you
tomorrow Your nothing can be great in their eyes They
need no one besides you for your smiles 186

SAFFIATOU JOOF

As a smart narcissist that scares only you Such depressing
personnel

Better please yourself out.

187

86. TICKLING MY PEN

It takes time and memories

That my hands once bleed

Nurturing them on a white silver elite To write these
suffice words of love My hair was cut shuttle

Gracious of the bald head

Fun it was , *'Lelibop'* I was mocked But murder the name
with new birth frames That become the place, the source of
my drawer key Hate could recal but can't do it to my skin
Who am I not to be riffed with cold foe?

I guess not, but truth remains to be my toe so But before
your finger prints my name Bait my words with a *hiqima*
of honey I was never in your physical schedules But you
can lay multiple eggs of my mirror That's not, shal not be
written on my thick skin But remember

Your conscience shal never sleep.

188

87. NO RUSH TO CHOOSE

They gave you names

When they knew, they were not capable They cracked you
for some days When they knew that

140

They couldn't break through your wal They said you are difficult

Because you sound too technical They tried to bring you down

Words are not now sufficient

When they make you believe

Just a little focus the pattern would change True love is not trained; you can catch its terrace They make you look old

Because al they dream is to make you a fool The time is not done

Because my grey hair hasn't shown Take your time, even if your hair gets you to the tail It is you alone living under that mirror Prayers are your weapons.

189

88. THE ALKAMBA TIMES ANNIVERSARY

In September last year

We promised you a Media change Our team is trending

We peck the neck of information In terms of online news

The Alkamba Times has proved Surviving the test of time

You can browse through

Get several roots to the news That brings the tights of truth As special from the crew

We inform, we translate

With the best content tool

Exposing the deception

A freedom space with no intimidation Lodging to our anniversary

As we refused to publish unjustly Get your glass of juice

We top the nation

Giving you advance news

190

SAFFIATOU JOOF

This is our passion, as we spil ed Fear not, touch the click button Let's scroll, roll our eyes

The Alkamba Times we can trust.

191

89. HER PRIDE

The feminine thing in her

Long roasted wigs

Long fresh legs, perfect edges Nails wel earthly shaped

Earrings are glittering, like mammy water The perfume fragrance heals

The heels so windy with gil s Hi, can I talk to you?

She blurred, nodded, she meant no sign He walked, talked,
and then cal ed She tried out, I have no time Message
hangs for days he believes But drifts seven times

Then watch her clock, no reply Ringing, she ignored, after
more days The phone cal begins

She has missed the ring tone

I was busy, behind with a big smile Dying to see the texts
like the moon flash

"Oh dear, sorry, I missed your cal s"

192

SAFFIATOU JOOF

No, she didn't miss any cal s She was indeed in love

But had to bluff for a while

My gender can counter-play movies Her pride, respect her
price.

193

90. MEN TOO HAVE A HEART

Coward, agree without being aggressive Struggling,
hauling, and craving to be loved A self-torturing mind he
has been Giving al , last for horrible seconds Bitterness, oh
hel of love in five minutes Tasteless, subdued for society to
question him Dared not speak of the heat he felt Not being
given enough sneeze he was hurt For al his suffering turn
into talks He complained, he wailed, he was mad, they said
I mean you hurt his nerves

Her sweet smiles are only poisonous Her beauty is sickening to betrayal remarks Don't put al your eggs in one bag She has no apex appetite for your love Quit, slowly for your mental health Men too cry alone, they too have a heart.

194

91. DON'T BE CONFUSED

The soul search for what the mind can control Then search not for the perfect being The birds are pecking through the window Hoping to spring on their source of grains But the short bird has perished in his dreams Keep the realms on what you can drink Marriage is a reality, set not like a footbal field Oh! Stubborn future of who was told Compete for a less limited time you spent Aspiring to be polish gold

Oh! Women, in God alone, you should console Change of endurance without haste to choose.

195

92. SO DARKEST SKIN

Cocktail bottle shaking

Can we share the table?

Ask for the waitress to come without regret Frowning faces hail for a distance To whom she might keep as a guest Worried for al I care

Judge not their minds

A crush I heard

Finding my soulmate

Get even much closer to my palms I shift my whole body,
scared of what?

Look at me like it's interesting Trembling so darkest skin

A torch light to ginger my body I am a free adult, buttress
fearing nothing Adjust to my comfort zone of love Turn
your strongest back on me I can't keep my eyes close for a
second The melanin thickness, quite featuring I am a
general lover of dark skinned girls 196

93. THE BLACK EMPIRE

Where we belong as a generation The true tattoos of a
black African man Defending and representing our
lineages From the smal est part of West Africa yet with
power A powerful employ look of the coastal areas Very
accommodating to set the records To hear the drums
beating the red hat The African descent wax ranged from a
distance Looking for a bucket full of water Springing its
energy

On an African stage

Tel ing one story of how to stand up The routine honours
glittering in his skin The black melanin being bolding The
black emperor in him shapes Displaying the replica of
Kunta Kinteh The kingship he would handle to his last
breathe You have headed a full country, a full nation That
you took an oath for your country Rainbow would be
formed from your fountain.

197

94. SHE IS PRICELESS

She woke up early to satisfy your needs The appealing appetite for breakfast awake She cooked your best choice of food Took bath and wore her finest sheets of cloth Her eyes were ordinary keeping you in prison The gliding of her structure was beautifully gifted Her angelic legs crossed quality at point She spread her trusted bed with white cotton From sunrise to sunset, she would check on you The low life she hosted, the shyness she chose Given you the best children shared between In her mistakes, she subdued with cool smiles Obedience she maintained, calm refined moves Come to rebuild your home with no il intention She embraced a private life, secretly coded close Intel igent she arose, your business wel handled Her in-laws, she adapted and deeply cherished The faith she believe religiously praised Smoked not, joked too, clever enough 198

SAFFIATOU JOOF

When in hardship she consoled your soul Her language was soft like the rabbit in pleasure.

Kept her close to your heart.

199

95. OUR UNIQUE DIFFERENCE DOWN

SYNDROME

On an afternoon dew point

She experienced the difficulty Of living with down syndrome

Left alone in the dark

A genetic disorder was marked She never was named in a book of love For our naked eyes, shouted through the world Giving her names, laughing at us But they are human like us

Just a distinctive pattern of physical characteristics A short stature in their life changed Within a period of time

Our support vanished through thin air A world we could have built

Their inclusion in society was limited We term to forget them

Is it a deliberate act?

Because their inability should not be a curse Rather a source to help boost them 200

SAFFIATOU JOOF

For they are not just a season The reason God gave them the extra chromosome Should be the reason to assist them But some are locked up in our world Waiting for miracles to feed them al Saddened by the situations, we left them We are al servants of God

None of us should be left alone Their progress may be very slow We require that extra care

Don't show us the weakness in your eyes But the strength of your spirit We are the joy of every household For al the time we need not only prayers For al the time, I watch our pretty hopes There is a shade in our body

There is a place in our soul

The volume, we are concerned, is your space Never to lose the grip we hold.

201

96. I AM GAY

Born this way

I try to change my natural identification Gist, I succumb to the nightmares of my dreams At times I fight with my pil ow To see that nature accepts me Yes, I change my hairstyles

The speed of my voice speech

In front of the camera I smile But its rare to feel the gay pride That comes with a price

I cannot change the green grass to yel ow Nor would I be able to change the pen to paper Left alone in a green nation the gay man cried But I hope to see him change his mind and For them to see that it's not pride but an act of being confused

I know that love is about heart not parts But remember that you can't beat nature apart I stand with the assurance that it's a violation of nature's rights

Breathing its atmosphere yet being ungrateful 202

SAFFIATOU JOOF

Granting you the chance to walk Dance and give you edible fruits It al ows animals to multiply To provide you with meat

But you're polluting our culture with lifeless men Walking under the heat of toothless gum When animals are busy producing babies Human beings are busy abusing nature I rise to speak for nature whose children are betraying its trust

Closing their hands with forbidden things And refusing to enjoy what is right Allah has cursed them an enduring punishment This is not like a tournament game But it would be tormented, scary and regrettable So their deeds on earth would be worthy but worthless on the hereafter

Purify the heart like a fresh leaf For Allah does see al

You might hate my words today But when the days are numbered and they are reminded

203

UNDER THE SPELL OF POETRY

You wil remember my words someday Nature deserves a transforming freedom Darkness is a gay man

Walking with full sight but blind Because you are

With the wrong age, wrong skin and wrong nose.

204

97. RISE TO YOUR FLAG

Make sure it never gets lapse Our situations, our crisis, wil
ever be our highlights Too dark to sit and to look at it get
deep It won't be there thrown into the bin Pouring blocks
in our homes

In order to get us to soak

Those days have passed

When our eyes were blind

It's a must built with our gums Let's treat each other like
neighbours That wil wear the same clothes Our shoes that
we should polish To expose any fake leader

205

UNDER THE SPELL OF POETRY

Your work must be shown to our eyes Or your words wil
be shredded Rise in these difficult hil s Nothing can dril us
real

Our youths have migrated

But their souls haven't left home Until our last breath, we
must rise to the flag My Gambia, our Home.

206

98. REMEMBER

A remarkable day for celebration Being marked as part of
the calendar That comes with a fresh deliberation The
Gambia arose from being in prison We grip to the branch
of freedom That rains into a liberated nation It was one
needle that stitched our lives Tribalism was packed aside
like token bread But our people forget

Too soon of the bonded reasons That put us together like a
pearl of bee pleasure That shrinks in our sensational hearts
It was one voice singing the song of freedom The Gambia
Smiling Coast, the strength of readiness Watching the
clock as its ticking we press The acceleration buttons to
kick dictatorship away Truly those days would remain been
memories 2016 forever it shal be inked I salute the genuine
fighters in that ring.

207

99. DHL SHIPPING COMPANY

Living under the shade of DHL

Breathing its fresh aroma from the environment The tree
spreads through its height Branding what its best looks in

151

the skylight Proceeding to revolt its greatness into the star
Like a wavelength displaying its beauty The destiny to
make your choice glimpse DHL has been an excel ent team
Since its existence with quiet techniques Contact our office
in short user miles Cease your fright due to its professional
might The innovative shipping

With better quality safety measures All are world leading
shipping express All are unique, even the blind can see the
goodness Do feel the ascending, DHL is trending The best
shipment that you can ever access Together you can trust
our business Fewer weeks with your shipment That is
guaranteed worldwide

208

SAFFIATOU JOOF

Our service is lifetime support Easily available for you to
earnest The standard is only set for progress Safely
protected

We dare not misplace your properties The records are
equal y set

With an undoubted success

Changing the face of the world We wil never stop bringing
smiles to your doorsteps.

209

100. DEMBO'S SPRING ROLLS

I have known your hands, how they works Your restaurant
I spend

With the rhythm of my poems

You have been a great mentor to my sight Giving me what
my late dad would have brought You hold a space in my
heart that I cal I cannot sleep without praising your kind
You saw me from a flat I never thought Made me your
daughter out of harm You have passed al the struggles of
my life You are my inspiration where I draw some clause
Wiped my tears when I needed it most 210

SAFFIATOU JOOF

Taught me what a daughter has to learn Be among the greatest people of my life To tel the world

Your space is unoccupied.

MR DEMBO GASSAMA

211

101. ULTIMATE CHEF

Where could I have been without you?

More than a sister I have dreamt to see As a toddler you never relented to impress me Giving me stories of my days at childhood You have shown me love and true sisterhood I made you cry but taught me how to write The best flavours I have ever been fed You shaped my mind and corrected me To al the jokes you painted in my closet The sisterhood pride you have built in me Furnished me secretively for the world to benefit Never was afraid to tel you how I felt Never was afraid to tel me the truth When I was wrong

My foresight came true because of your help You encouraged my talent

Encouraged me to break al barriers And final y get to chase my stream 212

SAFFIATOU JOOF

My flower would forever flourish with you Your flavors in kitchen are my strength Thank you **MARIAM SULAYMAN JOOF**.

213

102. BEST FRIEND

I heard her down so special to my soul A friend, a partner
we have been chosen Up to the mountains, my curtain she
has been Our past never defined our bedrooms Our family
tights are second to none A worker frame, our inspiration
we ever tamed Just found you as treasure close to me Hold
my hand beside your cheeks To the island we shal ever
mark In the beautiful pool of love we shal swim And your
love wil remain forever FATOUMATTA KIJERA

214

103. LOVE YOU MOTHER

Stuck to my roads, they did the pavement smooth Quick,
dark side, our mothers nurture us deep With clear belief as
a girl child Whose world was swal owed and steeped They
tiptoed in to uplift us

They gave us the best breast milk That no other human can
bring Taught and guide

And gave us a world of might

In their darkest twilight

They never blinked to change towards us Memory lane of
hardship came

Everything they dreamt was to make us gain Their worries
were subtle tide But their love remained the same Nine
months, a mother in pain They could have lacked the
appetite They could have lost their lives 215

UNDER THE SPELL OF POETRY

But their love kept us alive

Felt with no il effect

Embracing the love of brightness They are the stone

That every child should never throw To your heart, keep them closer to it.

216

104. IMAM TOURAY & IMAM FATTY

Wil I always say they have to be honoured?

Yes!

Or must I forward their legacy?

Yes!

For my generation to take notice of their works Almost
every young person

They have put knowledge in your sack Who would have
got

The guts to cry over the band of the Muslim hijab When its
issue was on the alert Imam Fatty came to strike the truth
upright How many schools that

They changed towards the sunrise Spreading the dawah
like an ample of a torchlight 217

Arm themselves with safe

And usual phrases of the Quran Perhaps the deen gained an impact through their reminders

They never forsake it like a fal ing apple When you mask to deny the future the truth Or you mask to stiffen their deen mission You shal perish

Because their leadership is with merits If an empty bottle rises to make some noise Its aim would be towards destruction Remember

These imams have built pil ars of the construction That makes Islam in the Gambia honoured When I rolled in the arch of the Island I felt proud of their work in our land.

218

105. WITH HER SUPPORT

How can an empty temple preach?

How would have been without her little efforts?

Stuck me with the wil to learn Sacrificed al her lively pleasures That warm words of her advice are precious Monitored al I shal ever get involved in Just to give me a life of treasure I never realized how the world would benefit Just to be touched with my own destination Pray to be a sea that her boats would float on That she raises me to be a full temple That my world would shine upon me as I confess **THANK YOU KHADDIJAH JOOF.**

219

106. NEVER COME ACROSS HIS KIND

OUSMAN MANJANG

The lethal of his words born to support Many youths have clung to his fingers That he redid with faith to uplift their grace That orbit to tense the atmosphere He's the lorry of the youths not a bicycle Reviving the lost spirit of the country Never longing for a fal

With him, even your moon shal recal 220

Drowsing eyes stirring the tree That possessed the future of our lives Reccurring the progress of his projects To put a smile on the faces of the earth He would never drown our skil s away Instead to awake the horns of our talent.

221

107. HE TEARS HER WATER

Penetrated her part she refuted Burst her water melon forcefully Grief for what she ever protected Her precious can never be replaced Haven't you got the humility of her price Stop to seek her pouches weak Distance apart let her be herself Trusted her to enter night and moon Let her be free

Let her faith be free

Let her body be free

Let her thoughts be free

Wait for her yes instead of your joy Don't force her to break her watermelon.

222

108. LOYAL TO YOU

I am around, ever since in my mind Never forsaking any of your errands I am here, ever compiled with errors Nowhere, you have seen me as vulnerable You show me ways how to stand out honourably Verily, I wil claim what is mine Verily, I promise to be forever yours Verily, my hands are here for you to take Verily, you know that I always care Verily, I have nothing hidden but to share Withhold, your kingship I crave Withhold, your tough body I gaze Stiffening, your words stil echo in my ears I am ready to wipe off your tears Have your seat in the corridor of my bed Have your secrets buried in my stomach Protect you like a snail laying her eggs.

223

109. AS A FUTURE CHILD

I didn't regret how I was controlled The limited time spent on phones And the hours that I was forced on my books The house control method of the daily calendar Time for everything, even jokes have a limit The tiny clothes I explored as a little girl Sometimes I look into them as fabulous Everyone doubts if ever she would wear a veil That love for food was immense in my name Instal ation of better western education But contained by religious principles as a guide By guiding my road to the future That I am already riding

In the peaceful way of Islam, I was raised Understanding who you are was a scale Blended with a Pan African mind I was trained With so much hype, less access to outings I thought that I was in a cage Little do I come across as lively?

A child that was monitored in the game of life 224

SAFFIATOU JOOF

Thought wel that maybe I was not being loved But now I am the family's favourite daughter A generation that I was prepared to face After they shaped me to be brave in mind A liberation that I identify my features I can present to tel my mum, "I'm ready to love"

Now that the world is in my control Parents have rendered their freedom of duty For I can't pay them enough of my salary I can't pay them off my difficult behaviour That they managed to formulate my future But I am going to love them forever as grace To tel you one more time that "Mum I love you"

Funny that I wil be handed over to someone Who also was searching for a girl to love Funny that they had prepared me To become a mother

To give the best for the society they crave In order to become a great exemplary person Listen to the wisdom of your parents There is love in everything that they structure
225

110. I KNOW

I know, you're not far

I know, you're just shy

I know, you're already mine

But the distance keeps us apart I can wait a couple of miles

Soon, you wil be near to my palms I know, upon seeing this, you wil smile That even if the dust gets into my eyes That love shal never evaporate to the sky It runs through my veins and within my heart.

226

111. YOU AND I

Locked up in the looming penetrating rays of the sunlight

And wake up to a surprise cal from the guitarist That beat the bowls

that strung against the kora

Tel ing us the ancestors that we came from In sweetness, in calmness, and in the most melodious voice of the griot

Shal ow the *tama* to belt it on his waistband to cal the shots of the island

That vibrates through the mangrove swamps to say one word of our names

The bird groups, sing it along as lonely val eys appear In the forest that shocks the snake to hiss The frog to jump, the lion to uproar And the sheep to run for its life You and I!

Pauses for the wrapper thrown at us The traditional wear that we owe to curse betrayal trials

227

UNDER THE SPELL OF POETRY

Revitalizing the most secretive spores of the body to be seen

The aroma experience

To feel the phrase that was makeable of the clan to distance ourselves from that scourge This sensation, this formation, and the second deem light

That our hands cherish, our minds bind Urging us to remain silent from the inner heart that is freezing down with so much energy to clear the rough life

You and I!

You can come to that stream

You can, could appear in my dreams You can float to the
periphery You can find me on the seashore You can get to
the gear of the stirring You can see me tal to the order of
your energy You can once more tel me, is this lust or love?

228

112. TRIBUTE TO LATE MARIAMA JALLOW

Mariama came for a mission

Left us shocked out of words

Quite short period of time

Built a legacy out of boldness Her death from the earth

Left us with a strong thought That my pen freezes with
tears Married without a kid

Mourning her out of grief

Cal ing her my favourite wife She has final y slept

Too deep to praise

Her serious initiatives

By the mercy of Allah

We pray our last word of peace Death has taken you away

But we shal never change our trails.

113. BUBACAR BOB KEITA

On a daily twilight, on a standing trial, He was wildly
accused of rape and kept remanded in mile two prisons for
two years He became a reason for our pen never stopped
dancing nor got drained

While his fans painted his name on defence

Innocent until proven guilty

The Gambian refused to believe, Bob became a trend

His fans rose to sing the song of freedom Free Bob, free
Bob, freedom to Bob 230

Even on a burning firing staunch In the hottest sunny
atmospheric wave bangs Like a beam of ray, his liberty

was ceized Aim to tarnish his image, with no breathing
space Bob was dragged to court

Lost almost al his close acquaintances Being bul ied as a
chance, to tarnish his lineage His business collapsed, but
his innocence kept him on alert

Scolded for a crime he didn't commit Maximum security
tightened, people got frightened, Prayers rained, when on a
trial, Bob was chased Even a toddler would sing that praise
Like a sharp needle piercing every artery The whole
Gambia went on shaking But his faith never gone forsaking
That was a thought that I have recal ed Thoughtful of al
prayers come to light This is our strive, end injustice in our
land Beyond the view of his case

231

UNDER THE SPELL OF POETRY

The crowd keeps increasing in one strife In his pearly
African caftan the judge ruled That cooked the goose, and
Facebook became a tool Free Bob, Free Bob, Freedom to
Bob.

When sunset, the DNA was sent to Ghana Truth returned
not to be in mystery A paternity test was introduced That
resulted in acquittal and discharge A further clean end on
the stirring news That cage, not Bob, was like a missile
blown in the air

That flake of orange feeling repels He's not the father

At last, eternal freedom on earth.

232

114. THE LOVE STORY

My heart is bleeding for the tragic story Out of many young women, he closed his eyes to your choice.

Out of patience, he was coaxed to the beauty And fought to build the bridges at no cost Between the dens of age, she burst feathers, Too scared of love results in little fruits Cracking the bridge of families that now scattered He surrendered to the pil ows of love He promised to keep you at your taste He planted the biggest mangrove cal ed source He even gave you the roses

The gifts from Banjul

Out of frustration, the friction got broken Then addiction to anger conflicts not frozen But he couldn't sleep

He couldn't eat,

He couldn't walk

There was a case with the prison shade He was paid a big price for being accused raped 233

UNDER THE SPELL OF POETRY

Atmospheric reshuffled, injustice revolted The pain of flimsy stories

Then married objectives confused with an obsession This resulted in a lost child during the race The various querries, mistrust for the victim The division of thoughts, minds, and hearts While with our alignment, the dust rejuvenated The story streamed like a wildfire The state to put a match for

the DNA test Without fear or favor of judgments deal For
over two years case, being adjourned thirty-three times

Oh! Hail for justice being delayed Oh! Wail for the
judiciary in question We wil al rise, cal ing for justice's
upper hand For the faith of Bob

This story could be scammed

And have never been spoken on a genuine ground When
shal we heal the wounds being open?

A nation with bruises of injustice Married wet leaves drop
to yel ow 234

SAFFIATOU JOOF

Where Banjul's redemption of love went apart A bridge of
love has gone to space.

235

UNDER THE SPELL OF POETRY

KEY GLOSORY WORDS

Tal Ataaya ; To brew green tea Lebon lu pain : Once upon
a time Amon naafie daana am;It used to happen before

Alkamba;

Is a village name in The

Gambia.

Jinns : Satan

Biri biri ; He was a great national football player in The Gambia.

Immam; A religious leader

Hamham; knowledge

Xalam; A traditional musical instrument Nha dua ying Cairo: We pray that about the peace

Fo Hakili tenko ning haar jeeba; With a peaceful mind and huge blessings.

Na koora julo: The string of my "kora"

Na musu fingo: My black woman Na musu koyoo: My fair woman

Deen; Religion

Kaaba : Mecca

236

SAFFIATOU JOOF

Kabaa: African spicy fruit

Te du foroh tol: it won't be bitter Neckut borrom hol : It's not a hot tempered person

Alla jelow: laughter

Naa galow: My girl

Fansorrow: showing up

Al kaa kele : fighting

Nha Fele ; looking

Haral Ma doh rek: I walk

Dila defaal chekesso : cat walk Nyepetor : Cockroach

Lelipop: bald head

237

Faiza's
Kitchen

CONTEH JULA

BRIDGE PROPERTIES

Fashion
Essentials
7474395/3907720
Address: Pipeline, The Gambia

KERR
FATOU

Star

tv

EXPRESS

Gach Group

KERR FINDER

KEXX NEWS

FINE tv
YOUR VIEWPOINT

LEIGH PROPERTIES

TASTE OF AFRICA

MSJ
Bureau De Change Ltd.

JOLUV
ARTS ENTERTAINMENT

100.4CAPITALFM

THE FATU NETWORK

INDIVIDUAL SPONSORS:

Zainab Musa Darboe (Jainaba Darboe) Seedy P Fofana

Sainey M.K Maraneh

Dembo Gassama

Sajoe Darboe

Ousman Manjang

EMPOWERED BY

238

ABOUT THE AUTHOR:

Saffiatou Joof was born to Sulayman Joof and Fatou Cham.

She attended Deeper Life Primary & Upper Basic School, proceed to Gambia Senior Secondary School in Banjul, where she graduated as a pure science student and got enrolled at the American International University West Africa in which she is currently studying computer science.

Joof is a poet, who started writing at an early age.

Saffiatou has been known for her determination and dedication as a poet to take poetry to another level. In 2014, she was among the team that represented Gambia in the 55th Olympic Mathematics Competition in South Africa and published her first poem about Africa in 2015

that gained her strength in poetry. Her articles have been shared by various media houses online in The Gambia.

She is the first Gambian poet that delivered a poetry reading at President Adama Barrow's Inaugural day on 19th January 2022. An inspiring young woman, who is currently the President of Stand Stil Organization, The Gambia (SSOTG) that focuses on its advocacy on civic enlightenment. Saffiatou is also the founder of virtual poetry network and the host of The Poetry TV Show that showcases talent and culture. She has been shortlisted for the Momodou Sabal y spoken word poetry for the year 2022-2023 and currently the poet of *The Alkamba Times* featuring a story about "The Arrogant King in the Vil age".

Her website www.nnakalavirtualpoetry.gm

www.ingramcontent.com/pod-product-compliance
Lightning Source LLC
Chambersburg PA
CBHW051832150726
47998CB00001B/390